# 1999 IRON TALK'S
## ANTIQUE PRESSING IRON
# PRICE GUIDE

**Plus:**
1995-1996-1997-1998 IRON TALK Index
Categories for Iron Collectors
Secrets of Cleaning Irons
Basic Iron Collecting
Advanced Iron Collecting

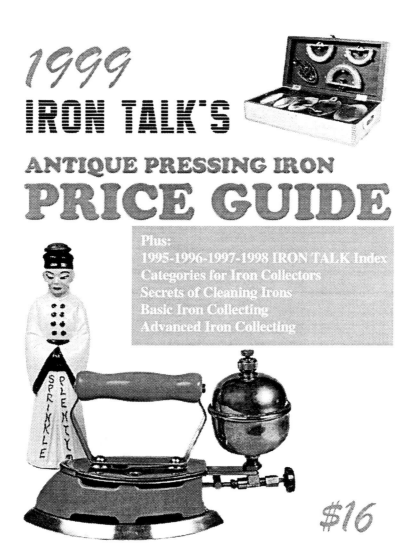

$16

**By Carol and Jimmy Walker**

ISBN 0-9667867-0-X

© 1998 Carol and Jimmy Walker
P O Box 68
Waelder, Texas 78959

# Table of Contents

Introduction ........................................................................................ iv

How to Use This Guide ........................................................................ 1

The IRON TALK Category Codes for Iron Collectors ........................... 2

1999 Prices ......................................................................................... 5

Secrets of Cleaning Irons ................................................................... 26

Basic Iron Collecting .......................................................................... 31

Advanced Iron Collecting .................................................................... 37

1995-1998 IRON TALK Index .............................................................. 47

Back Issues ........................................................................................ 69

How to Subscribe to IRON TALK ......................................................... 71

# INTRODUCTION

Why do you need a price guide for irons? What's the problem? If a price is asked, you're free to pay it or not. Negotiation may be successful— words often change the outcome. Or you can walk away and hope to find the iron somewhere else. The market isn't perfect. Antique irons aren't sold like bread and milk. Ten dealers may ask ten different prices for the same piece. What's the point of a price guide? It's a jungle out there.

This is exactly why a guide is needed. Prices are all over the map, too high, too low or whatever the market will bear. Dealers often charge according to what they paid—or what they imagine an iron is worth. Unless they are experienced in the field, either method is likely to be closer to a guess than the actual value.

You need someone counseling your side when the going gets tough. It's your money and you don't want to spend it foolishly. You should take advantage of all the help you can get. If a guide can suggest an appropriate scope of values, it's smart to pay attention to it.

Dealers have problems related to the other side of the coin. They want to avoid paying too much for inventory and they're interested in selling it for a fair price. Specialty dealers understand the need to hold prices within the accepted range. But a dealer who is only casually involved with irons usually doesn't have a clue.

Either way— for dealer or collector, buyer or seller—a price guide can be helpful and sometimes essential.

Prices are a regular feature in *IRON TALK* and are well-accepted by most readers. They understand that this source supplies the background they need to be informed. However, it's hard for readers to locate prices scattered among different issues. Time makes a difference, too. Prices change. This separate updated volume is needed to consolidate prices. They are in order and with the most recent quotes. And, because this is a companion to *IRON TALK*, it contains a comprehensive alphabetical index of subjects from 1995 through 1998.

Publishing a price guide for pressing irons is a risky business. The editors understand that many collectors (and some dealers) are offended by published prices. It's as though they are pretending that irons aren't bought and sold. Perhaps they make believe that irons come from the Easter bunny.

Nonsense, there is a vigorous market for antique pressing irons.

And, like all markets, it has prices that are always changing. The hobby is maturing and it's earning recognition for its importance. While some pieces can still be found in the five to twenty-five dollar range, there are exceptional irons that now rival the prices of other established collectibles.

Some object to our listing current prices. Of course, we regret their decision. However, it's their opinion and they're entitled to it. Their reasoning isn't clear, but it appears to be the desire to keep everything a secret. We wonder what the attitude might be if they were collectors of coins, stamps, tools or depression glass—all with extensive price guides.

The editors take a different view. We favor dissemination of information. Knowledge is power. Our readers deserve to have every advantage we can offer. Prices aren't a secret. They are constantly revealed in auctions, price lists, antique publications, the Internet and in other public offerings. We were dealers for ten years. We have served as price advisors for two respected price guides. We maintain a constantly updated computer database of prices. Because we know a little about the market in antique irons, we feel it's our obligation to share it with our readers.

It's our job to report prices, not to establish them. This market, like all others, is driven by supply and demand. It's simply classic economics. More and more people are chasing fewer and fewer irons. This is why the market trend is up. And, unless, the laws of economics are repealed, it will continue in an upward movement punctuated by fits and starts, plateaus and surges, with unexpected fads contributing to the erratic movement.

Geography makes a difference. The same iron may bring dramatically different prices whether it's sold in Europe, America or Australia. This price guide deals only with values in the United States. Even so, the geographical differences can be significant even within the same country. North or south—east or west—markets are different and prices vary with the local conditions. Some dealers make a good living buying in one part of the country and selling in another.

Even the time of the year can make a difference. The off season, usually in mid-winter, may prompt dealers to trim asking prices. However, during the height of the antique selling months, irons usually bring top prices.

Aside from the overall buoyant price movement, individual irons are valued by four powerful factors:

**1. Age.** The older the better. But age isn't everything with irons or other collectibles. A comparatively recent Elvis Presley record is worth more than an ancient Enrico Caruso 78 RPM. It's the same with irons. Age is only one factor to consider.

**2. Scarcity.** How many have you seen? How many are known to exist? This is important, but one-of-a-kind irons frequently are underpriced because a market history doesn't exist.

**3. Condition.** A beautiful iron is a joy to behold. Expect to pay more for top condition.

**4. Desirability.** This is the final element in the equation. It's the most difficult to define, but can best be explained as the "I gotta have it" factor. Never underestimate the power of desirability.

Price information in this guide is restricted to one line. A range of prices is given instead of a single inflexible number. Usually, the market price will lie somewhere between the lower and higher price. Be aware that every factor contributing to the price isn't shown. *IRON TALK* is not responsible for errors. To protect us from unwarranted litigation, it's necessary to include the following disclaimer:

*IRON TALK* intends to supply information reflecting an accurate range of prices as found in today's market. Prices aren't absolute. This is only a guide. Ultimately, the correct price is the amount agreed upon by a willing seller and a willing buyer. *IRON TALK* shall not be held responsible for losses or damages of any nature caused or alleged to be caused by information contained herein.

# How to Use This Guide

This price guide is different from any other you ever used. It's designed especially for the iron collector. The coverage is restricted to pressing irons and related collectibles. You won't find carnival glass, graniteware, furniture, Barbie dolls or any other categories that are standard flea market offerings. Those things are handled elsewhere. This is a guide for people who care about irons. It doesn't attempt to establish prices. Instead it simply reports the current prices of collectible irons sold in malls, flea markets and private sales across America. Many of these prices are stable over a period of time while others (particularly the unusual and rare) sometimes take sudden leaps in value.

This guide is divided into categories. A rational division is necessary to provide a vehicle for organization. Reference material must be designed for quick and easy use. A guide is no good unless you can find what you are looking for. However, to be effective, any variation from a standard alphabetical listing requires some education of the reader.

"The IRON TALK Category Codes for Iron Collectors" is used as a medium for listing various iron types. This code is based on mnemonics to help you remember them. As an example, "Billiard Iron" is categorized as "BI." In some cases,

strict adherence to the mnemonic system would cause duplication. Then a little special effort is required to recall the code. This is particularly true in subcategories. A good example is "Trivet, Iron" that uses the code "TN." In this case, "Iron" is represented by "N" to avoid conflict with "TI," used for "Tie Press." Review the list and pay attention to the structure offering easy memorization. When there's a departure from the expected, a brief explanation is always supplied. After a little practice, you'll find the category codes suggest themselves without taking time to look for them.

Use the list of category codes as a table of contents to find the page number you're seeking in the Price Guide. By thinking in categories, you'll avoid the mental gymnastics of wondering whether an iron will be found under country, type, company or material. For the most part, the category code is a two-letter designation. If it's a charcoal iron, you'll find it listed under "CH" whether it's from Germany or Indonesia, nineteenth or twentieth century, iron or brass, made by Grossag Company or Bless & Drake. This simplifies your search and gives you instant information.

Little irons are in a special category using the "L" prefix. The section on little irons in "The IRON TALK Category Codes for Iron Collectors" explains the organization

of little irons by handle designation and by smaller versions of full-size irons.

We strongly recommend "The IRON TALK Category Codes for Iron Collectors." Use the codes to find current prices. Become comfortable with them and leave yourself open to understanding the beauty and simplicity inherent in this method of organization. Try it, use it, you'll love it. Take the Category Codes into your heart. Use them for your own collection. You'll find your records will be easier to manage. You can inventory your collection, categorizing your irons in a reasonable and simple system. For more on how to do this, see Issue No. 16 "Record Keeping for Iron Collectors."

If you recognize the importance of irons in history—if pressing irons are at the core of your life—this Price Guide is for you.

# The IRON TALK ®
## Category Codes for Iron Collectors

Full size irons use a two-letter code plus numbers. Example: Egg irons would be EG-1, EG-2, etc. The example of fluters is explored in the cover story of **IRON TALK** No. 16 "Record Keeping for Iron Collectors." Fluters are divided into three groups: Fluter, Fork (FF), Fluter, Hand (FH) and Fluter, Machine (FK for Fluter, Crank). Notice the mnemonic use of key letters and sounds to help you recall the codes. Little irons have "L" before the code.

**Accessories**       **AC**

Not for irons. Examples: handle pads, waxers and spare parts.

**Advertising**       **AD**

Not for irons. Examples: signs, magazine advertisements, printers' blocks, tobacco cutter.

**Advertising Iron**       **AI**

Irons with advertising. Primarily used for little irons (LAI).

**Ball Iron**       **BA**

**Billiard Iron**       **BI**

**Book**       **BK**

**Boxed Set**       **BX**

**Box Iron**

Box irons are divided according to lift gate style. See *Iron Talk* No. 2.

| | |
|---|---|
| Box Drop In | **BD** |
| Box Lift Gate | **BL** |
| Box Lift Out Gate | **BO** |
| Box Lift Top | **BT** |
| Box Scottish | **BC** |
| Box Swing Gate | **BS** |
| Box Swivel Gate | **BW** |

Note that Scottish "BC" and Swivel Gate "BW" can be remembered by similar sound.

**Cap**       **CA**

Full size irons only. Little irons are Oval or Round Back.

**Card**

| | |
|---|---|
| Postcard | **PD** |
| Trade Card | **TD** |

**Ceramic Iron**       **CI**

Primarily used for little irons (LCI).

**Charcoal**       **CH**

**Combination**

Combination irons have more than one purpose.

| | |
|---|---|
| Combo, Box | **CB** |
| Combo, Charcoal | **CC** |
| Combo, Reversible | **CR** |
| Combo, Sad | **CS** |

**Detachable Handle**       **DH**

**Egg**       **EG**

**Electric**

| | |
|---|---|
| Electric, Deco | **ED** |
| Electric, Other | **EO** |

**Figurine**       **FI**

## Flower

| | |
|---|---|
| Flower and Leaf | **FL** |
| Flower Shaper | **FS** |

## Fluter

| | |
|---|---|
| Fluter, Fork | **FF** |
| Fluter, Hand | **FH** |
| Fluter, Machine (Crank) | **FK** |

## Fuel

| | |
|---|---|
| Fuel, Alcohol | **FA** |
| Fuel, Petroleum | **FP** |

## Gas: Natural and Carbide    GA

Not to be confused with gasoline.

## Glass    GL

## Goffering

| | |
|---|---|
| Goffering Iron | **GO** |
| Goffering Stack | **GS** |

## Hat    HA

## Heater    HE

## Jewlery    JE

Iron related jewelry.

## Linen Press    LP

## Little Irons

Little irons add the "L" prefix to the two-letter system of full size irons. Example: a full size detachable handle uses the code "DH" while the little detachable handle is "LDH." Little sad irons, however, are identified by the grip-type nomenclature introduced by Judy Politzer. Example: little cross rib is "LCR." Exception as used by Politzer: base takes precedence over handle type. Example: little round-back cap with a strap handle is "LRB."

## Little Sad Irons

| | |
|---|---|
| Block Grip | **LBK** |
| Creature | **LCE** |
| Cross Hatch Grip | **LCT** |
| Cross Rib Grip | **LCR** |
| Curled Handle | **LCU** |
| Cylinder Grip | **LCY** |
| Diamond Grip | **LDI** |
| Enterprise | **LEN** |
| French | **LFR** |
| Hollow Grip | **LHO** |
| Miscellaneous | **LMS** |

Not defined by any other category.

| | |
|---|---|
| Open Rolled Grip | **LOR** |
| Oval | **LOV** |
| Replaced Handle | **LRH** |
| Rod Handle | **LRD** |
| Rope Handle | **LRP** |
| Round Back | **LRB** |
| SolidCast | **LSC** |
| Strap Handle | **LSR** |
| Swan | **LSW** |
| Tri-Bump | **LTB** |
| WireHandle | **LWI** |
| Wood Grip | **LWO** |

| | |
|---|---|
| **Mangle** | **MA** |
| **Mangling Board** | **MB** |
| **Miscellaneous and Novelty** | **MN** |

Related but non-iron items.

| | |
|---|---|
| **Mushroom** | **MR** |

**Pan Iron**

| | |
|---|---|
| Pan, China | **PC** |
| Pan, Greece | **PG** |
| Pan, Korea | **PK** |
| Pan, Philippines | **PP** |
| Pan, All Other | **PA** |

| | |
|---|---|
| **Patent Model** | **PM** |

Takes precedent over other category codes. All types of patent models, are coded "PM" whether sad, fuel or otherwise.

| | |
|---|---|
| **Plaiter** | **PL** |
| **Poking Stick** | **PS** |
| **Polisher** | **PO** |
| **Primitive** | **PR** |
| **Replaced Handle** | **RH** |

**Reproduction (R") suffix to normal code.**

Example: "Sad Iron" is SA. Reproduction Sad Iron" is SA(R)."

| | |
|---|---|
| **Reversible** | **RV** |
| **Sad** | **SA** |
| **Seam** | **SE** |
| **Sleeve** | **SV** |
| **Slickenstone** | **SS** |
| **Sprinkle Bottle** | **SK** |

**Stove**

| | |
|---|---|
| Stove, Gas | **SG** |
| Stove, Fuel | **SF** |
| Stove, Laundry | **SL** |
| Stove, Salesman Sample | **SP** |
| Stove, Toy | **ST** |

| | |
|---|---|
| **Tailor and Commercial** | **TA** |
| **Tie Press** | **TI** |
| **Travel** | **TR** |

All types of travel irons, are coded "TR"whether sad, fuel electric or otherwise.

**Trivet**

| | |
|---|---|
| Trivet, Brass | **TB** |
| Trivet, Iron | **TN** |

"Iron" is represented by "N" to avoid conflict with "TI," used for Tie Press.

| | |
|---|---|
| **Trousers Press** | **TP** |
| **Uncategorized** | **UC** |

For irons not fitting into any other category. Non-iron items not fitting into standard categories are coded Miscellaneous and Novelty "MN."

# Prices

## ACCESSORIES  AC
See **IRON TALK** Issue 14 "Iron Cooler"

Iron cooler ............................ 150.00-200.00

## ADVERTISING  AD
See **IRON TALK** Issue 5 "Poster Stamps"

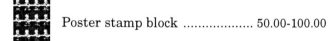
Poster stamp, iron related ............ 5.00-10.00

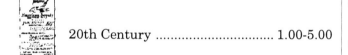
Poster stamp block ................... 50.00-100.00

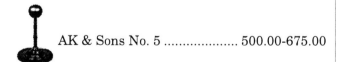
20th Century .............................. 1.00-5.00

## BALL IRON  BA
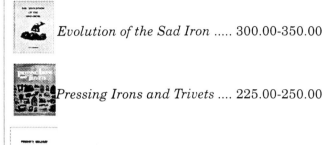
AK & Sons No. 5 .................... 500.00-675.00

## BILLIARD IRON  BI
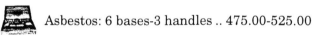
7¾" ......................................... 160.00-200.00

## BOOK  BK
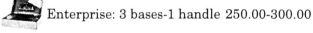
*Early Tuesday Morning* ........... 40.00-50.00

*Evolution of the Sad Iron* ..... 300.00-350.00

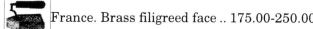
*Pressing Irons and Trivets* .... 225.00-250.00

*Tuesday's Children* .................. 75.00-100.00

## BOXED SET  BX
Asbestos: 6 bases-3 handles .. 475.00-525.00

Enterprise: 3 bases-1 handle 250.00-300.00

Enterprise: 5 bases-3 handles 500.00-700.00

## BOX IRONS
See **IRON TALK** Issue 2

### DROP-IN  BD
Belgium. w/brass trivet. ....... 600.00-750.00

France. Alsace-Lorraine ....... 300.00-400.00

France. Brass ...................... 200.00-300.00

France. Brass filigreed face .. 175.00-250.00

Handmade roundback............ 700.00-900.00

## Lift Gate BL

 Brass and steel. Lyre gate 1000.00-1500.00

 Brass and iron, scroll gate  800.00-1050.00

 Brass. Denmark ..................... 90.00-110.00

 Brass, dolphin uprights ........ 250.00-300.00

 Brass. Guided lift gate ......... 150.00-250.00

 Brass. Turned uprights ......... 125.00-200.00

 England. Brass sole ............. 150.00–250.00

 England. 18th century ........ 100.00-150.00

## Lift Out Gate BO

 Brass. Dolphin uprights ....... 200.00-300.00

## Lift Top BT

 Siddons ................................... 55.00-150.00

## Scottish BC

See **IRON TALK** Issue 13

 Arrowhead "S" supports ... 2000.00-2500.00

 Copper & brass grip ....... 2500.00-3000.00

 Gothic "S" supports ........... 2500.00-3000.00

 Plain "S" supports ............. 1500.00-2000.00

 Rotating handle ................ 2000.00-2400.00

## Swing Gate BS

 Brass. Dated ........................ 300.00-500.00

 France. 18th century ............ 300.00-500.00

## Swivel Gate BW

 Cold nose ............................ 300.00-500.000

 Goffering pin. Leather grip .. 600.00-900.00

 Ox-tongue, brass ................... 100.00-175.00

 Ox tongue, porcelain handle. 600.00-800.00

 Ox-tongue, single post.......... 100.00-150.00

## Top-Hinged Gate

 D'Eye and Rowlands ............ 700.00-900.00

## Cap CA

 Sylvester #6 ............................ 30.00-40.00

# CARDS

## POSTCARDS PD

 Flatiron Building .................. 7.00-10.00

 Flat Iron Girl .................. 10.00-15.00

 Common. .................. 10.00-20.00

 Rare .................. 25.00-50.00

## TRADE CARDS TD

See **IRON TALK** Issue 11 "Mrs. Potts Advertising Trade Cards"

 "And the raven answered" ....... 35.00-60.00

 "Arrival of Enterprise Iron" ... 75.00-100.00

 "Dog as iron, man jumps fence" 35.00-60.00

 "Expedition to the North Pole". 25.00-35.00

 "For China Direct" .................. 35.00-60.00

 "I go up and you go down" ........ 45.00-75.00

 "In De Colored Folk's Heaven" . 25.00-40.00

 "It was a darling, so it was"........ 35.00-60.00

 "Jumbo" .................. 45.00-75.00

 McLaughlin's Coffee ................ 20.00-30.00

 "Melican Man".................. 20.00-25.00

 "Mrs. Florence Potts" .............. 20.00-30.00

 "Mr. Toodles!" .................. 30.00-50.00

"President and Mrs. Hayes" ... 75.00-100.00

"Sad Iron Outfit" (3 bases) ..... 75.00-100.00

"Sad Iron Outfin" (5 bases)... 100.00-150.00

"Sad Irons" (hand holds iron) . 75.00-100.00

"Sad Irons" (woman ironing) .... 50.00-75.00

"Scene Just Outside Cowville" . 25.00-35.00

"So says Uncle Sam!" ................ 35.00-60.00

"The Children Cry For It" ........ 25.00-35.00

"The Ladies Favorite" ............... 35.00-60.00

"The Wedding Present" ............. 30.00-50.00

"Three Chinese in laundry" ...... 45.00-75.00

"They all want it" ...................... 45.00-75.00

"Uncle Sam: China/California"  45.00-75.00

"Virtue Shines Brightest" ......... 25.00-40.00

"You'll find it everywhere" ........ 45.00-75.00

# CHARCOAL IRONS CH

See **IRON TALK** Issue 1, Issue 10 "Brittany Charcoal"

Demark. "Gemo" ..................... 80.00-100.00

France. Brittany 1700's. ......... 450.00-600.00

France. Clothespin latch ..... 400.00-500.00

France "Liberty Cap" ............ 400.00-600.00

France. Common .................... 50.00-100.00

France. w/Snail latch ............ 400.00-600.00

Germany. "Berliner" .............. 600.00-800.00

Germany. Dalli. ..................... 100.00-150.00

Germany. Dragon chimney 1000.00-1500.00

Germany. Griffin latch .......... 200.00-400.00

Germany. Lion's head latch .. 150.00-200.00

Germany. Max Elb. . .......... 1200.00-1500.00

Germany. Rooster latch ........... 75.00-100.00

Germany. Rooster latch ........ 125.00-150.00

Germany. Vulcan. ................. 500.00-800.00

India. Brass. .......................... 100.00-175.00

India. Brass, large ................. 100.00-175.00

Indonesia. Brass .................... 125.00-150.00

Indonesia. Brass, w/dragon .. 135.00-200.00

Japan. Revolving chimney ... 125.00-200.00

Japan. Revolving chimney ... 125.00-200.00

Mexico. Pagoel ...................... 25.00-35.00

Mexico. Porcelain, dove latch . 75.00-175.00

Mexico. Tisa ............................. 25.00-40.00

Portugal. Split chimney ....... 225.00-325.00

Sweden. Husqvarna ............ 800.00-1100.00

USA. Acme Carbon Iron .......... 75.00-100.00

USA. Bless & Drake .................. 50.00-65.00

USA. Chimney ........................... 40.00-50.00

USA. No. 4 pin release top ....... 50.00-70.00

USA. Improved Progress ....... 100.00-200.00

USA. Ne Plus Ultra ............... 200.00-275.00

USA. Onlyone ....................... 150.00-200.00

USA. Onlyone 1914, 1916 .... 100.00-150.00

USA. Onlyone June 7, 1932 . 100.00-150.00

USA. Peerless Self-Heating .. 150.00-200.00

USA. Taliaferro & Cummings ... 100.00-200.00

# COMBINATION

## BOX IRON/FLUTER  CB

Streeter patent ........................ 750.00-900.00

## CHARCOAL/FLUTER  CC

Pease with Trivet .................... 500.00–600.00

Classen patent ........................ 300.00–400.00

## REVERSIBLE  CR

See **IRON TALK** Issue 4 "Reversible Combination Irons"

"The Champion" ............... 1000.00-2000.00

"The Economist" .................... 500.00-700.00

"Family Laundry Iron" ......... 500.00-700.00

Fox .......................................... 600.00-800.00

Hewitt, no bed ....................... 200.00-300.00

Hewitt's "The King Iron" ...... 500.00-800.00

"Ladies Friend" w/bed .......... 700.00-900.00

Mann's. .................................. 175.00-275.00

Patent 1876 ........................... 700.00-950.00

Young, Hewitt and Mooney .. 700.00-950.00

## SAD IRON/FLUTER  CS

Charles Anderson, Pat. 1871 100.00-150.00

Knapp patent w/toe latch. ..... 125.00-160.00

"Little Giant" ........................ 500.00-700.00

F. Myers, Pat. 1871 ............... 375.00-500.00

# DETACHABLE HANDLE  DH

Asbestos Pat. 5/22/1900 ............ 25.00-45.00

Bless & Drake bentwood ....... 200.00-250.00

Colebrookdale ........................... 25.00-35.00

Enterprise, double point ......... 25.00–35.00

Enterprise, square back .......... 50.00–60.00

Griswold set of 3 ................... 100.00-150.00

Harper set of 3 ...................... 200.00-275.00

Ober, size 1 .............................. 50.00-70.00

Sensible No. 4 .......................... 50.00-70.00

Wapak set .............................. 85.00-125.00

Weida w/thumb release ........ 250.00-300.00

# EGG IRON  EG

Tommy Iron w/attachment ........ 200.00–250.00

With tripod stand ...................... 300.00–350.00

9

# Electric

## Electric , Deco ED

Silver Streak, Saunders .. 1200.00–1500.00

## Electric , Other EO

American Beauty, Pat. 1908 .... 20.00–30.00

Graybar ...................................... 25.00-35.00

Various names, Pat. 1905 ......... 35.00-50.00

Winchester ............................ 100.00-150.00

# Figurine FI

"Flat Iron Girl" 8-inch .......... 500.00-800.00

Girl holding ironing board ...... 85.00-100.00

Girl in yellow hat ...................... 50.00-65.00

"Girl Ironing" ......................... 250.00-400.00

"Girl with Iron," Lladro ........ 400.00-500.00

Ironstone Decanter ................. 85.00-125.00

Laundry maid .......................... 40.00-50.00

"My Chores," Lladro ............. 325.00-350.00

Older lady ironing ..................... 45.00-60.00

"Press On," Precious Moments 75.00-100.00

# Flower FL

Brass and iron ........................ 75.00-100.00

# Fluter

See **IRON TALK** Issue 5 "American Fluter Irons"

## Fluting Fork FF

Five fingers ............................... 15.00-30.00

## Hand Fluter FH

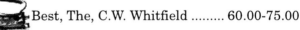American Machine ................ 110.00-150.00

Best, The, C.W. Whitfield ......... 60.00-75.00

Block Press ............................. 90.00-140.00

Clark .................................... 125.00–150.00

Doty, Perkins patent ............ 275.00–375.00

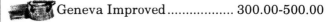Geneva .................................... 35.00–55.00

Geneva Improved ................. 300.00-500.00

Howell Wave ...................... 425.00-500.00

Olmsted, lever operated ..... 750.00-1000.00

J & A McFarlane ...... 250.00-350.00

J. Ponton .............................. 150.00-200.00

Shepard No. 65 ..................... 175.00-225.00

Shepard No. 70 ................... 175.00-225.00

Shepard No. 75 Separate bed 135.00-185.00

Shepard No. 85 .................... 125.00-175.00

Shepard No. 98 w/box ...... 175.00-225.00

Sundry .................................. 300.00-350.00

## MACHINE FLUTER FK

American Machine ............... 110.00-150.00

Cole Counterweight ................. 450.00-600.00

Crown, North Bros. .............. 110.00-150.00

Dudley ................................. 550.00-750.00

Eagle, full-size, 5½" rollers ... 100.00-150.00

Holmes patent .................... 900.00-1000.00

Imperial .............................. 300.00-500.00

Knox ..................................... 150.00-200.00

"Knox, The Original" w/photo 450.00-600.00

Manville Feb. 23, 1869 ....... 900.00-1000.00

Peerless ................................. 200.00-275.00

Tucker, Pat. Feb. 7, 1871 ...... 300.00-400.00

# FUEL

See **IRON TALK** Issue 9, Issue 17

## ALCOHOL FA

Alcomtic Iron, Pat. 1923 ....... 250.00-325.00

Feldmeyer w/trivet .............. 100.00-300.00

Rotary Iron, Adamson's ........ 125.00-175.00

## PETROLEUM FP

Acron Brass Mfg. Co. ............ 500.00-600.00

All British Pumpless ................. 45.00-75.00

American Gas Machine ........ 175.00-275.00

American Gas Machine ........... 50.00-70.00

American No. 66 ........................ 6000-85.00

Best Yet, The ......................... 500.00-750.00

Coleman 1 ............................. 200.00-300.00

Coleman 2 ............................. 175.00-250.00

Coleman 4A ............................. 50.00-75.00

Coleman 4A with accessories . 75.00-100.00

Coleman 4-A Canada ............... 45.00-60.00

Coleman 4-E ......................... 250.00-350.00

Coleman 5 .............................. 90.00-125.00

Coleman 12 ......................... 150.00-200.00

Coleman 615 ......................... 100.00-150.00

Coleman 615A ...................... 100.00-150.00

"Diamond, The" ......................... 30.00-50.00

Early, no markings .................. 40.00-60.00

"Hydrocarbon" ...................... 200.00-300.00

"Imperial" ............................... 75.00-100.00

"Improved Easy Iron" .............. 50.00-90.00

J.F. Casey & Co. .................... 175.00-225.00

"Jubilee" No. 9 ...................... 175.00-225.00

Monitor, front tank .................. 45.00-75.00

Monitor, streamlined model ..... 50.00-70.00

Montgomery Ward ................... 40.00-50.00

National Stamping Co. .......... 85.00-100.00

"New Leader" ........................ 250.00-350.00

"Nonpareil, The" ................... 100.00-150.00

"Peerless" .............................. 200.00-300.00

"Perfecto" .............................. 150.00-250.00

"Rex Hydrocarbon" .............. 200.00-300.00

Royal front tank ................... 100.00-150.00

Royal Model D ......................... 50.00-75.00

Royal, The, front tank ............. 45.00-60.00

Sears 5947, pump in handle... 85.00-125.00

Sears 5988, pump in tank ...... 85.00-125.00

Sette, Pat. 1913 ...................... 90.00-130.00

Slant handle ......................... 250.00-350.00

Standard .............................. 175.00-250.00

Standard, Mansfield Ohio .... 250.00-300.00

Sun ...................................... 100.00-190.00

Sunshine .............................. 200.00-300.00

Tilley, England ..................... 150.00-175.00

"Wonder Iron" ........................... 50.00-75.00

"Wonder Iron," w/pressure gauge 150.00-200.00

# GAS GA

## NATURAL AND CARBIDE
See **IRON TALK** Issue 7 "Special Gas Irons"

Beetall ................................. 250.00-350.00

"BUDAPEST" ...................... 190.00-275.00

Colt, carbide ........................... 50.00-70.00

Decorated, Germany .............. 90.00-110.00

Decorated w/stove, Germany 200.00-250.00

Enameled stove, France ....... 150.00-190.00

"Eureka," England ................ 150.00-200.00

Improved Otto, England ....... 100.00-150.00

"Jewel," USA .......................... 200.00-300.00

LaRue Nu-Styl .................... 250.00-300.00

LaRue Nu-Styl w/weight ... 450.00-600.00

"Laurel Fletcher" .................. 200.00-300.00

Upright on stove, Belgium ... 150.00-190.00

With rear door .......................... 40.00-50.00

# GLASS IRON GL

Sun Flame ........................... 300.00-450.00

# GOFFERING
# IRON GO

See **IRON TALK** Issue 10 p. 10 "Goffering Machine"

Porcelain barrel ................. 500.00-600.00

Serpent upright................... 900.00-1200.00

Two barrel monkey tail .... 1500.00-2000.00

# GOFFERING
# STACK GS

13½" high.............................. 120.00-175.00

# HAT HA

See **IRON TALK** Issue 8 "Whatsit? Foot Tolliker,"

Issue 12

Band block ................................ 20.00-30.00

Band block stretcher ............... 40.00-50.00

Brim iron ............................ 125.00-175.00

Brim iron ............................ 125.00-150.00

Brim iron ....................... 60.00-80.00

Cav iron .................................. 90.00-125.00

Crown creaser ...................... 125.00-150.00

13

Crown iron ........................... 250.00-300.00

D'Orsay curling machine ..... 125.00-175.00

Hot water iron ...................... 400.00-500.00

McDonald/Knox Rotary Iron 300.00-400.00

Puller down ............................. 35.00-45.00

Rounding jack ......................... 40.00-60.00

Runner down, brass ............. 100.00-150.00

Runner down, wood ................ 40.00-50.00

Shackle ................................. 100.00-150.00

Shackle, detachable handle .. 250.00-300.00

Shackle, hinged .................... 150.00-190.00

Shackle, large curl ............... 125.00-160.00

Shell, electric ....................... 50.00-75.00

Shell, gas ............................. 150.00-200.00

Shell, slug ............................ 175.00-225.00

Tolliker, 3 groove .................... 90.00-125.00

Tolliker, concave ................... 150.00-190.00

Tolliker, duckbill ................... 100.00-125.00

Tolliker, foot, aluminum .......... 75.00-100.00

Tolliker, foot, brass ............... 120.00-190.00

Tolliker, foot, iron ................... 75.00-100.00

Tolliker, foot, wood ................... 65.00-90.00

Tolliker, front and rear ......... 175.00-200.00

Tolliker, heart ...................... 120.00-175.00

Tolliker, offset ...................... 125.00-175.00

Tolliker, offset ...................... 100.00-150.00

Two-handle gas ........... 300.00-400.00

# HEATER  HE

"Centennial, The" Pat. 1876 . 300.00-400.00

Charcoal. Clay covered w/tin 100.00-200.00

"Dessau," Germany ........... 3500.00-4000.00

French. Holds 3 irons ........... 500.00-650.00

"Garland Sad Iron Heater" .... 90.00-150.00

"Globe" Pat. July 5, 1881 .... 200.00-300.00

"Golden Star" holds 3 irons 200.00-275.00

"Monitor" holds 2 irons ......... 150.00-200.00

"Mora," Czechoslovakia .... 1500.00-1900.00

Natural Gas .......................... 250.00-350.00

"Potter, M.F." Pat. 1850 ...... 500.00-600.00

Pyramid, holds 3 irons .......... 140.00-175.00

Single, stove top ................... 100.00-150.00

Triple, stove top .................. 200.00-300.00

# JEWELRY  JE

 Charm, silver, Enterprise ......... 30.00-50.00

 Charm, silver, Geneva fluter .... 50.00-60.00

 Charm, silver, Scottish ........... 75.00-100.00

 Charm, silver, Swan ................. 50.00-60.00

# LINEN PRESS  LP

 Napkin press .................... 1,500.00-1700.00

# LITTLE IRONS

See **IRON TALK** Issue 3

## LITTLE ADVERTISING  LAD

 Paperweight, Cockshutt. ... 200.00-250.00

 Paperweight, Reid Bros ..... 225.00-275.00

 Tailor iron. 3¾" ..................... 175.00-250.00

## LITTLE BLOCK GRIP  LBK

 Number 1, Scarce 2⅞" ........ 100.00-140.00

## LITTLE BOX IRON

### LIFT GATE  LBL

 Brass, 3¾" embossed "1735". 450.00-600.00

### SWIVEL GATE  LBW

 Ox tongue w/slug 1⅞" ................. 75.00-90.00

## LITTLE CAP

 English. Fine casting. 3⅞" ... 625.00-725.00

## LITTLE CHARCOAL

 Indonesia. 3½". ...................... 100.00-175.00

 Portugal. Split chimney 4" .... 600.00-900.00

 USA. Chimney pin latch 3¾" 800.00-1100.00

## LITTLE CROSS HATCH

 Nickel and gold paint 3 ¾" .......... 50.00-75.00

## LITTLE CROSS RIB  LCR

Number "4" on grip. 3⅝" ............ 35.00-50.00

## LITTLE CURLED HANDLE  LCU

Closed curls. 2¼" ........................ 35.00-50.00

Open curls. 2⅛" .......................... 50.00-75.00

## Little Cylinder Grip LCY

 Double point. 3" ......................... 35.00-45.00

 Spade-shape, uncommon. 2¼". 75.00-100.00

## Little Detachable Handle LDH

 Enterprise Centennial. ⅞" .... 500.00-600.00

 Meyers 3⅝" ............................ 125.00-200.00

 Potts type, unmarked 3⅓" ........ 65.00-85.00

## Little Diamond Grip LDI

 3 ¼" ............................................. 35.00-50.00

## Little Fluter

See **IRON TALK** Issue 7 "Little Fluters"
### Hand LFH

 Crimper, Dutch ..................... 150.00-200.00

 Crimping board w/tongs ........ 350.00-500.00

 Geneva 3½" x 2" ............... 1000.00-1200.00

 Neep, brass, Dutch ................ 125.00-175.00

 Tiny rocking fluter 1⅞" ........ 600.00-800.00

 Tinier rocking fluter 1⅜" ... 800.00-1000.00

### Machine LFK

 Eagle raised name 3½" ........ 400.00-550.00

Eagle stenciled name 3½" .... 400.00-550.00

## Little French LFR

 Flower on face. 3" .................... 80.00-125.00

 Lot of 4, 2¼"—4" ............ 450.00-600.00

## Little Hollow Grip LHO

 Flower on face. 3¼" .................... 40.00-60.00

## Little Linen Press LLP

See **IRON TALK** Issue 8 "Featured Iron: Linen Press"

 20½" tall ............................. 2000.00-2500.00

## Little Misc and Novelty LMN

 Matchcase. Silver plate. 2¼" . 225.00-275.00

 Needlecase. 2½" ..................... 100.00-175.00

Saccharine container. 1⅝" ........ 50.00-75.00

 Wood pattern, Williams trivet .. 25.00-50.00

## Little Open-Rolled Grip LOR

Star on face. 3 ½" ...................... 30.00-50.00

## Little Rod Handle LRD

 Ober 4" half round ................. 100.00-175.00

 Thick base. 3 ¾" ........................ 50.00-75.00

## LITTLE ROPE HANDLE LRP

Nickel and original paint ........ 35.00-45.00

3" ................................................. 30.00-40.00

Right hand twist. 2 ⅞" ......... 150.00-250.00

## LITTLE ROUND BACK LRB

Belgian unmarked. 2 ⅞" .......... 60.00-90.00

## LITTLE SCOTTISH LBC

with trivet ........................ 2000.00-2800.00

## LITTLE SLEEVE LSV

Arcade .................................. 300.00-500.00

## LITTLE STOVE, TOY LST

Bucks Junior 22½" ................ 200.00-300.00

## LITTLE STRAP HANDLE LSR

Unmarked. 3¼" ........................ 35.00-50.00

## LITTLE SWAN LSW

1¼" w/trivet ........... 900.00-1000.00

1⁵⁄₁₆" no paint ...................... 250.00-350.00

1⁵⁄₁₆" w/trivet, no paint ....... 275.00-375.00

1¾" w/ trivet, 50% paint .... 225.00-250.00

1⅞" w/trivet, paint traces .. 225.00-250.00

1¹⁵⁄₁₆" w/trivet, 90% paint ... 225.00-250.00

2⅛" w/trivet, no paint ......... 160.00-225.00

2³⁄₁₆" w/trivet, 80% paint .... 200.00-250.00

2¼" no paint ........................ 150.00-200.00

2¼" w/trivet, 80% paint ...... 200.00-250.00

2⅜" w/trivet, 80% paint ..... 200.00-250.00

2¾" original paint ............. 150.00-225.00

2¾" w/trivet, 90% paint ..... 200.00-250.00

2¾" w/trivet, lacks detail ... 125.00-175.00

2¾" w/trivet, brass ............. 250.00-300.00

2⅜" Folks Fescht 1941 ......... 85.00-100.00

3¼" Rara Avis ................... 800.00-1000.00

5" no paint ......................... 500.00-700.00

## LITTLE SWAN REPRO LSW(R)

1⅞" .............................................. 5.00-20.00

## LITTLE TRI-BUMP LTB

Smooth bumps. 3½" ................. 60.00-85.00

Spiral bumps. 3⅜" ................... 35.00-50.00

## Little Trivet ltn

Cathedral .............................. 15.00–25.00

Williams ................................ 25.00–50.00

## Little Trivet Repo ltn(r)

Taiwan ..................................... 5.00–8.00

## Little Uncategorized uc

Fancy design. 1 $\tfrac{5}{8}$" .................. 125.00-160.00

Portuguese w/trivet 1 $\tfrac{1}{4}$" ....... 125.00-200.00

## Little Wire Handle lwi

0 $\tfrac{1}{2}$" with trivet ........................... 55.00-85.00

## Little Wood Grip lwo

"The Victor 10" 3" ................... 125.00-175.00

## Mangle ma

Household Clothes Mangle 125.00-200.00

## Mangling mb

Horse handle ................ 1700.00-2000.00

Primitive Scandinavia . 900.00-1,200.00

# Miscellaneous and Novelty mn

## Misc. and Novelty: Banks

Flatiron Building 3⅜-inch .... 400.00-500.00

Flatiron Building 5½-inch ..... 200.00-350.00

Flatiron Building 5⅞-inch ..... 500.00-600.00

Flatiron Building 8¼-inch 2,500.00-2,800.00

## Misc. and Novelty: Glass, China and Porcelain

See **IRON TALK** Issue 2 "The Truth About Pressed Glass," Issue 5 "Candy Containers"

Candy container, Chocolade tin 65.00-85.00

Candy container, Rountree tin . 65.00-85.00

Candy container, electric iron .. 65.00-85.00

Candy container, flat iron ..... 600.00-700.00

Ox tongue ............................ 200.00–300.00

Glass butter dish. New ........... 75.00-100.00

Glass butter dish. Old ........... 200.00-250.00

Glass sad iron dish. New .......... 45.00-65.00

Glass sad iron dish. Old ........ 100.00-150.00

Royal Bayreuth baby cup ...... 125.00-200.00

Royal Bayreuth tumbler ....... 600.00-700.00

## Misc. and Novelty: Other

Ironing Monkey w/box ....... 200.00-250.00

Spoon, Flatiron building. .... 50.00-100.00

Tobacco cutter. ..................... 900.00-1100.00

Washing Machine 18" ........... 400.00-600.00

Wash Mitt, w/instructions ..... 75.00–100.00

## Misc. and Novelty Paper

See **IRON TALK** Issue 9 p. 10 "Comic Valentine"

Magazine cover, 1922 ............... 25.00–50.00

Valentine, iron related ............. 15.00–20.00

Valentine, comic, iron related .. 20.00–30.00

## Misc. and Novelty Photography

Stereoscope card ...................... 20.00-30.00

## Mushroom MR

On round wood base ............. 250.00-130.00

## Pan Iron
### Pan, China PC

Cinnabar handle ................... 225.00-275.00

Dark patina .......................... 175.00-200.00

## Patent Models PM

Bosom board, Pat. 1879 .... 1000.00-1200.00

Washing machine .................. 500.00-700.00

Reversible gas, 1877 ........ 2500.00-3500.00

## Plaiter PL

Singer Mfg. Co. ..................... 175.00-350.00

Wood and metal ........................ 30.00-50.00

## Poking Stick PS

Brass handle ................... 1,000.00-2,000.00

Simple design ........................ 600.00-800.00

## Polishers PO

Block grip w/cross ribs .............. 50.00-60.00

Camion Frères, France ......... 160.00-200.00

Enterprise, ventilated grip ....... 75.00-90.00

Gem ...................................... 350.00-450.00

Hood's Patent soapstone ...... 175.00-250.00

Mahoney ................................. 25.00-35.00

Mary Ann B. Cook ............... 150.00-200.00

Unmarked, smooth sole ........... 20.00-30.00

## Primitive  PR

Slave Iron. Jingle in handle ... 75.00-150.00

## Replaced Handle  RH

Sad iron, Sturbridge Village ..... 40.00-50.00

## Reversible  RV

"The Trent" naturlal gas ....... 500.00-600.00

## Sad Irons  SA

Belgium, flowers on face ........... 40.00-60.00

Belgium, w/trivet ................. 500.00-700.00

France, set of 5 ............... 150.00-250.00

France. L. Tillet No. 3 ............... 50.00-75.00

France, white porcelain .......... 75.00-100.00

Switzerland, single post ....... 240.00-300.00

USA. Average quality. ............... 15.00-20.00

USA. Common quality .............. 10.00-15.00

USA. Good quality. .................... 20.00-30.00

USA. Chattanooga ................ 100.00-150.00

USA. Haven & Co., dolphins .... 50.00-75.00

USA. Monitor 5 ..................... 300.00-400.00

USA. Soapstone 6 ⅜" ............ 200.00-250.00

USA. Ventilated slotted handle 50.00-75.00

Mexico. Brass handle ............ 100.00-150.00

Ober No.9 w/arched handle ...... 25.00-35.00

## Sleeve Iron  SV

Asbestos .............................. 175.00-225.00

Bless and Drake ....................... 40.00-50.00

Electric with trivet ................ 65.00-100.00

Duckbill, Pat. June 15, 1887 ........ 350.00-450.00

Ober ...................................... 65.00-80.00

Sensible No. 4 ................................ 50.00-75.00

Sensible No. 5 ................................ 50.00-75.00

## Slickenstone  SS

See **IRON TALK** Issue 15 p. 14 "Slickenstone"
Issue 16 "Slicken-or Rubbingstones"

Clear glass w/spiral in handle 400.00-500.00

20

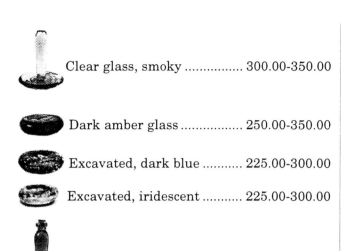

Clear glass, smoky ............... 300.00-350.00

Dark amber glass ................ 250.00-350.00

Excavated, dark blue ........... 225.00-300.00

Excavated, iridescent ........... 225.00-300.00

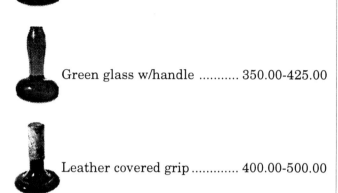

Green glass, mushroom shape 350.00-425.00

Green glass w/handle ........... 350.00-425.00

Leather covered grip ............. 400.00-500.00

Lignum vitae ........................ 300.00-400.00

## Sprinkle Bottle SK

See **IRON TALK** Issue 18 "Clothes Sprinklers"

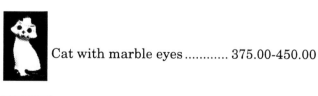

"Beer Can" ............................... 60.00-75.00

Cat with marble eyes ............ 375.00-450.00

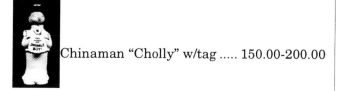

Chinaman "Cholly" w/tag ..... 150.00-200.00

Chinaman Emperor ............ 225.00-275.00

Chinaman holding an iron .... 225.00-275.00

Chinaman, removable head .. 375.00-450.00

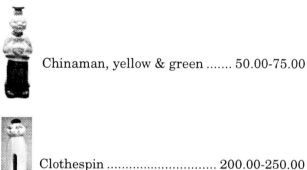

Chinaman, yellow & green ....... 50.00-75.00

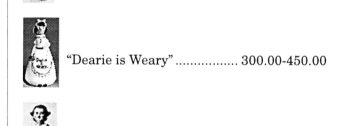

Clothespin ............................. 200.00-250.00

"Dearie is Weary" ................. 300.00-450.00

Dutch girl, wetter downer .... 200.00-250.00

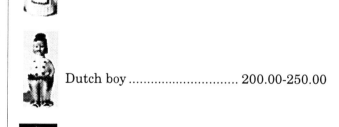

Dutch boy .............................. 200.00-250.00

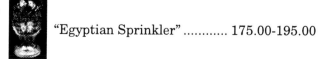

"Egyptian Sprinkler" ............ 175.00-195.00

21

Elephant, pink and gray ......... 90.00-125.00

 Elephant American Bisque ... 375.00-450.00

 Fireman, Cleminsons ......... 750.00-1000.00

 Glass bulb, hand blown .... 100.00-150.00

 Glass bulb w/label ............. 200.00-300.00

 Iron-shape, blue delft type ..... 75.00-100.00

 Iron-shape, lady ironing ......... 75.00-100.00

 Iron-shape, souvenir ............. 200.00-300.00

 Iron-shape, wetter downer 125.00-140.00

 "Lady Bug," plastic ................... 45.00-60.00

 Mammy "Mandy" old ........... 325.00-400.00

 "Mary Poppins," Cleminsons 225.00-300.00

 "Merry Maid," w/label .............. 40.00-50.00

 "Merry Maid," w/o label ........... 30.00-40.00

 Milk glass, molded ............. 90.00-125.00

 "Myrtle," Pfaltzgraff ............. 300.00-400.00

 Peasant woman ..................... 150.00-175.00

 Poodle .................................. 250.00-300.00

 Rooster, sprinkler version ..... 175.00-250.00

 Siamese cat, Cardinal .......... 200.00-300.00

 Sprayer, advertising ................. 50.00-75.00

 Sprayer, Wilkins ....................... 50.00-75.00

 Sprinkler cap, aluminum ............. 2.00-2.50

 Sprinkler cap, plastic ................... 1.00-1.50

Sprinkler cap, rubber stopper .. 10.00-20.00

 Sprinkler cap, snap on ................. 1.00-2.00

## Sprinkle Bottle Wana-bes
See **IRON TALK** Issue 10 "Not Quite Sprinklers"

 Boy, black pants ................................ 35.00

 "Carrie Nation" ......................... 15.00-25.00

 Girl w/doll, yellow dress .......... 7500-100.00

 Girl, yellow dress ................................ 35.00

 Mammy, new, white w/maroon trim .. 35.00

 Mammy, short w/green dress ............. 35.00

 Mammy, tall, white w/blue & tan ...... 35.00

 "Naughty Lady" ......................... 50.00-60.00

 Cleanser dispensers, pair ..... 130.00-150.00

 Decanter, Gobel elephant...... 175.00-250.00

"Kleanser Kate" ........................ 50.00-60.00

 "Kleanser Kate" unmarked ...... 40.00-50.00

 Merry Maid, glass, new ................ 20.00-25.00

 Pop bottle, converted .................... 4.00-7.00

 Queen ....................................... 50.00-85.00

 Salt and peppers, boy & girl..... 30.00-40.00

 Sprayer, plant .......................... 20.00-35.00

 Turnip/Radish, cruet ............... 50.00-85.00

## Stove
### Stove, Laundry sl

 France, 5 irons, 24" ......... 1,500.00-2,000.00

## Tailor ta

Geneva, Ill .............................. 40.00-50.00

## Travel Irons tv
See **IRON TALK** Issue 6 "Travel Irons"

### Alcohol

Iron and stove in oak box ..... 190.00-275.00

Iron and stove w/leather case 100.00-150.00

## Electric

3 ⅜" .......................................... 75.00-100.00

Baby Betsy Ross in box .......... 65.00-100.00

Betsy Ross, satin-lined case . 100.00-150.00

Hammered aluminum ............... 35.00-50.00

K-M Gad-A-Bout ....................... 10.00-25.00

Porcelain plugs 4 inch ............... 50.00-75.00

Steemco Steemette .................... 50.00-75.00

Sunbeam in metal case ............. 35.00-50.00

Toastmaster steam/dry ............. 25.00-50.00

Three prongs w/case ............. 100.00-150.00

## Electric Combination

Curling iron, side opening ........ 30.00-75.00

Hotpoint Utility Iron w/parts 300.00-500.00

Suitcase, mint condition ....... 500.00-800.00

Universal, w/curling iron ......... 45.00-60.00

## Gas Jet

Chalfant (hers) ...................... 250.00-350.00

Chalfant (his) ....................... 250.00-350.00

Elite, The ............................... 150.00-200.00

Gas or alcohol ....................... 200.00-275.00

Gem, The 3 ⅞" ...................... 250.00-350.00

McDonald/Knox Rotary Iron 300.00-400.00

Sultana Toilet Iron w/trivet .. 300.00-375.00

## Meta Fuel

Bugolette, multi-colored grip 140.00-160.00

Bugolette, white grip ............ 140.00-160.00

Fuluse w/trivet, fuel & box ...... 7500-100.00

Green wood grip w/box of fuel .. 45.00-60.00

In box w/instructions ................ 80.00-90.00

Revolving ............................... 100.00-175.00

Swiss ......................................... 45.00-60.00

## Meta Fuel Combination

Black wood grip w/curling iron 60.00-80.00

## Trivet
### Trivet, Brass TB

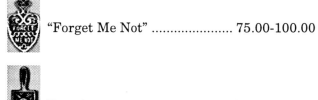

"Forget Me Not" ...................... 75.00-100.00

Rose in center .......................... 75.00-100.00

## Trivet, Iron  TN

Bunker Claney, Rest ................. 35.00-50.00

Hinged, for Pease iron .......... 100.00-150.00

Ober "OMCo." ........................... 15.00-25.00

Ober "Waffle" ........................... 20.00-300.00

Spider Web ................................. 10.00-20.00

## Trousers Press  TP

"Empire" in box ........................ 50.00-75.00

## Uncategorized  UC

Steamer for teakettle ............. 85.00-120.00

Wood pattern, Sensible sleeve . 50.00-75.00

Wood pattern, top and base ..... 50.00-75.00

Wood pattern, top plate ............ 25.00-50.00

Wood pattern, sq. back ............. 50.00-65.00

25

# Secrets of Cleaning Irons
## Looking good

The question asked more often than any other is "How can I clean my irons?" Here's the answer. First, be warned. It's not easy, it's not quick. You can damage your irons, ruin your clothes, and injure yourself. Be careful! Wear eye protection, old clothes, a protective apron and gloves. Some cleaning products are powerfully corrosive. Read these suggestions carefully with particular attention to the principle of using the least assertive methods that will accomplish the desired effect. If you splash acid in your eyes or discolor a prized iron, we don't want to hear about it. Don't come crying to us. This is hazardous work. We told you so.

*IRON TALK* shall not be responsible for losses or damage of any nature, caused or alleged to be caused, by following the information supplied herein. This is a legal disclaimer. We are serious. If you are doubtful about following these instructions safely, then have your irons professionally cleaned.

Each iron must be evaluated on a case-by-case basis. There's no one answer for all situations. If the first try doesn't work, do something else. Use the least destructive

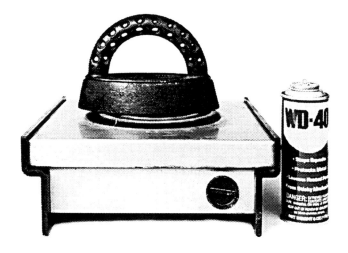

*Hot plate and WD 40 are essential for drying and seasoning irons after cleaning.*

*Products for final finishing include waxes, polishes and fixatives.*

methods first, extreme solutions last.

Perhaps we can agree that an iron collection is more attractive when the irons are dust free—dirt free—rust free. Brass is prettier when you can see the color. Irons should not show signs of abuse or neglect. They ought to be healthy and happy.

The first consideration is to begin with quality. Use discrimination in building a collection. It's better to spend time and money acquiring good irons than cleaning junkers.

Avoid replacements and repairs. These conditions are difficult to disguise or correct. Is the nickel or chrome finish rusted or damaged? Bright metal surfaces cannot be restored short of replating (usually an unsatisfactory solution). How severe is rust damage? Extreme pitting can never be reversed.

Cleaning must consist of the gentlest approach possible. If the case isn't extreme, a restrained touch is enough to produce the desired result. The objective is an iron that's clean, bright and happy. A well-cleaned iron invites handling and petting.

It's convenient to divide the cleaning process into four degrees of aggression:

**1. Non-aggressive.** Steel wool, washing, oiling, waxing.
**2. Somewhat aggressive.** Chemicals, steel wool.
**3. Aggressive.** Bench grinder, flexible shaft.
**4. Excessively aggressive.** Sand blasting.

When using chemicals and power tools, always wear eye protection and appropriate gloves.

### REMOVING PAINT

Non-original paint is removed before cleaning. You can tell the difference. Newer paint is often lumpy and uneven. It doesn't belong. Use paint remover for taking off repaint, but be careful to preserve original paint. Follow directions on the product. The paint removal process cleans the iron and prepares it for the washing steps listed below. Often the non-original paint was applied to cover defects. After it is removed, the iron can be evaluated. Decide what further steps are needed and proceed with the cleaning.

Methods follow, beginning with the least degree of aggression.

### NON-AGGRESSIVE
#### LIGHT RUST REMOVAL AND WASHING

Nothing is more gentle and effective for removing light rust than 0000 steel wool. This is a very fine grade. Anything coarser than 000 is not recommended because of the possibility of scratching. After rust removal, wipe clean using a cloth dampened with paint thinner. This may be all the cosmetic attention the iron needs. If so, finish with an application of wax and it's ready for display.

For washing, spray with Simple Green, 409 or Fantastic. Scrub with a soft brush, rinse under running water and dry well. Place on hot plate set at low heat to dry thoroughly. (A hot plate is essential for this purpose. Iron has a sponge-like structure that absorbs moisture. Heat drives out water.)

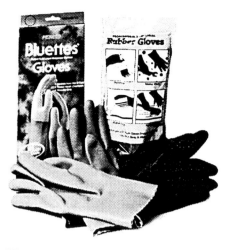

*Wear appropriate gloves: Bluettes household gloves for waxing, professional strength for chemicals.*

When dry, remove from heat, spray with WD 40, place back on the hot plate at medium heat to "season." The object is to fix the oil deep into the pores to prevent future rust. As a bonus, this usually imparts an attractive dark color resembling the natural hue of a well-used iron. Spray with WD 40 every 15 minutes during this "seasoning" process. After about an hour, turn off heat and allow to cool. Note: You'll be well advised to do this operation outdoors or in the garage. It produces smoke and smell. If done inside, it will pollute the house and set off the smoke alarm.

When cool, remove excess WD 40 by wiping with paint thinner.

Apply brown wax and buff. This will correct uneven color and soften the appearance. Spraying with non-glossy artist fixative seals the wax, prevents it from rubbing off and increases its life. Most people find the slight luster attractive. Be careful, a too-heavy application can look artificial. LPS Rust Inhibitor provides no color but may be used instead of wax if desired. Waxing is not permanent. Nothing is forever, so understand the waxing will eventually need to be redone. How often depends on conditions. Watch your irons. They will tell you.

*This seasoning method can be used for cast iron cookware. If there's cooked-on grease, remove it with a mild oven cleaner. Then wash well and precede with the above instructions, eliminating the use of all chemical products. CAUTION: Use vegetable oil on cookware instead of WD 40.*

### SOMEWHAT AGGRESSIVE
#### CHEMICALS FOR REMOVING RUST
BOILED LINSEED OIL AND VINEGAR

Charlie Herrick Jr. favors this old-time method. Brush off all light rust. Apply a mixture of one part boiled linseed oil and one part vinegar. Wipe off excess. Set aside to dry. Be patient, this is slow drying. Linseed oil is effective at preventing rust and offers years of protection.

UNSWEETENED LEMON LIME KOOL-AID

Bernie Rousseau passes along this method for removal of rust and corrosion. Nickel is mostly unaffected by this process but any parts coated with a porcelain finish will suffer badly. It takes the shine off porcelain and leaves a dull grainy finish. Keep it away from painted parts.

Use two small packages of

*Simple Green is the preferred cleaner. If not available, use 409 or Fantastic.*

unsweetened Lemon Lime Kool-Aid per quart of water. Only the *unsweetened* kind will do. Soak the pieces in this mixture three to four days. Periodically use 0000 steel wool on the article. Then return it to the solution. Repeat until the rust disappears. Heavily rusted parts will turn a silver-gray color. Bernie mentions that Coleman collectors are finding this method quite useful. He was skeptical until he tried it himself, but now he is a believer.

*A mild but surprisingly effective rust removal procedure involves the use of Lemon Lime Kool-Aid.*

EXRUST
   Caution:
      Do not use on painted surfaces.
      Do not use on porcelain surfaces.
      Wear professional rubber gloves.

Disassemble component parts, noting order for reassembly. Penetrating oil is useful for loosening stubborn screws. If not completely disassembled, at least remove the wood handle. If handle can't be removed, wrap securely with plastic wrap to protect it from chemical damage. Isolate all porcelain and painted parts. They'll be ruined by the chemical. Don't say we didn't tell you.

Make solution of EXRUST, according to directions on the bottle, to cover the iron. Immerse iron in the EXRUST solution. Soak, brush every 30 minutes or so with a steel bristle brush until rust is removed. Rinse with water and dry well with cloth. Then follow the hot plate "seasoning" method. Apply brown wax. Spray with non-glossy fixative.

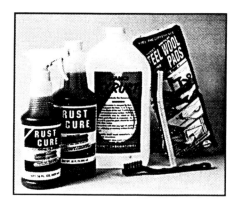

*Rust is enemy of iron collectors. Specialty products are helpful in its removal. This is strong medicine. Be careful.*

## PRODUCTS
These are the cleaners, waxes, chemicals and supplies mentioned in the text. Most are available in paint stores, supermarkets, small appliance shops, antique shops and builder supply stores. Specialty products are harder to find. See "Sources."

1. Washing products
   - Simple Green
   - 409
   - Fantastic
2. Cleaners and protectants
   - Paste wax, brown and clear
   - Glorifying-Antique
   - E-Z Shine Metal Polish
   - Jubilee Kitchen Wax
   - LPS Rust Inhibitor
   - Artist fixative, non- glossy
   - Boiled linseed oil and vinegar
   - WD 40
3. Penetrating oil for loosening screws
   - Kano Sili Kroil
   - Liquid Wrench
4. Paint thinner or mineral spirits
5. Semi-paste paint remover
6. Rust removal
   - Rust Cure
   - EXRUST
   - Unsweetened Lemon-Lime Kool-Aid
   - Steel wool, grades 000 and 0000
   - Steel bristle brushes
7. Brass cleaning
   - Ammonia
   - Lysol Toilet Bowl Cleaner
   - Jax Instant Brass and Copper Cleaner
   - Kwick Kleen Brass and Copper Cleaner
8. Equipment
   - Gloves
      Bluettes for waxing
      Professional for chemicals
   - Eye protection
      Safety goggles
   - Hot plate
   - Steel wool, grades 000 and 000
   - Wire brushes
   - Toothbrushes
   - Bristle brushes
   - Brass bristle brushes
   - Q-Tips
   - Rags
   - Heavy duty shop towels

RUST CURE
   Caution:
      Do not use on paint.
      Do not use on porcelain.
      Wear professional rubber gloves.
      Do not use any water with Rust Cure.
   Cover work surface with a plastic sheet.
   Spray iron with Rust Cure. Let stand 30 minutes, brush with a steel bristle brush. Spray again, let stand and brush. Repeat until rust is removed. Wipe off excess with a cloth soaked with paint thinner. DO NOT USE WATER. It forms a white film that's nearly impossible to remove.
   Let dry. Apply brown wax and buff. Spray with non-glossy fixative.

*Disassembly is encouraged before cleaning. Two penetrating oils that will loosen tight screws are Kano Sili Kroil and Liquid Wrench.*

### AGGRESSIVE
BENCH GRINDER FOR REMOVING RUST
   Use a bench grinder with a fine wire brush. Wear eye protection and gloves. This method has the danger of over cleaning, leaving the iron a bright gray. Also it is hard to get under handles and around uprights. A flexible shaft brush can be used for detail work but it is only good for small areas and is expensive. After buffing on the wheel, the brightness can be moderated with WD 40 in connection with the hot plate "seasoning" method. Follow by waxing and buffing.

### EXCESSIVELY AGGRESSIVE
SAND BLASTING
   Sand blasting is almost guaranteed to over clean, causing the metal to turn an unpleasant gray. Moreover, the surface will immediately begin to rust again unless protected. Sand blasters using glass beads are somewhat more gentle.

### OTHER MATERIALS
Wood handles, nickel, chrome, brass.

### WOOD HANDLES
   First wash and dry thoroughly. Then brighten and refurbish handles with these products.
   • Walnut or other natural handles: Use brown wax.
   • Black handles: Use black shoe polish.
   • Red handles: Use red shoe polish.
   • Blue handles: Use clear paste wax or Jubilee.

*Paint thinner is an all purpose solvent following a variety of products such as Rust Cure, steel wool, WD-40 and other oils.*

### NICKEL AND CHROME
   Everything classified as "somewhat aggressive" can be used to remove rust from nickel and chrome. The only difference is to use more dilute concentrations of EXRUST than is shown on the bottle. Leave EXRUST and Rust Cure on less time. Use 0000 steel wool to scrub the rust away. Remember NO WATER with Rust Cure. How many times to I have to tell you?
   The Lemon Lime solution is even gentler. But watch closely.
   Polish nickel and chrome with metal polish, follow with clear paste wax or Jubilee Kitchen Wax.

*Brass requires special treatment using products suited for its unique characteristics.*

### BRASS
   Caution: Use a brass bristle brush. Brass won't scratch brass. If cleaning fluter rollers, remove rollers from fluter. Wear professional safety gloves.

### NON-AGGRESSIVE
   Wash with full strength ammonia, using brass brush.

### SOMEWHAT AGGRESSIVE
   Pour Lysol Heavy Duty Toilet Bowl Cleaner into a plastic pan. This is messy. Keep the solution in the pan and be careful of spills. Saturate item with cleaner, scrub with brass brush until clean. Rinse and dry.

## SOURCES

This is where to find specialty products. *IRON TALK* has no connection, financial or otherwise, with these companies. The editors do not sell these products and cannot function as an ordering service. For more information, contact the companies directly.

BRIWAX Paste Wax
dark brown, light brown, oak and clear
    Phone: 1-800-5 BRIWAX

E-Z SHINE Metal Cleaner
    Phone: 1-800-356-1022

WENOL all-purpose metal polish
    Williams-Sonoma

RUST CURE
    TRI-WIN
    PO Box 5274
    Waco TX 76708-0274

EXRUST
Sili Kroil Penetrating oil
    KANO LABORATORIES, INC.
    1000 S. Thompson Lane
    Nashville, TN 37211-2627
    Phone: 615-833-4101

JAX Instant Brass and Copper Cleaner
    JAX CHEMICAL CO., INC.
    78-11 267 St.
    Floral Park, NY 11004

KWICK KLEEN Brass and Copper Cleaner
    KWICK KLEEN INDUSTRIAL SOLVENTS
    PO Box 807
    Vincennes, IN 47591
    Phone: 812-882-3987

*A clean iron is a happy iron.*

### AGGRESSIVE
JAX Instant Brass and Copper Cleaner. Saturate and brush until clean. Rinse and dry.

### EXCESSIVELY AGGRESSIVE
Kwick Kleen Brass and Copper Cleaner. This is very strong. Scrub with cloth. Rinse and dry.

Note: The last three products may turn brass pink. This is a chance you take. There are no guarantees in life. Polish can sometimes remove most of the pink color. A cloth wheel on a bench grinder used with buffing compound produces a professional polish on brass.

### FINAL TOUCH
After cleaning and polishing with any of the above methods, finish with E-Z Metal Polish. Then wipe with Glorifying Antique. This removes any white residue and provides an invisible protective film.

If you've followed these methods, you've expended time, effort and money. Your irons are looking swell. But will it last? It depends on how you take care of them. Improper storage can ruin all your work. Temperature changes cause condensation on irons. Garages and basements are the worst offenders. Irons don't like the cold and damp or the heat of summer. They want the same living conditions you do. Give them an environment of stable temperature and low humidity. They'll love you for it. How to do it? Move them into your living quarters. Or provide heat for the collection. Install a humidifier. You figure it out.

### THAT'S IT
Your babies are all cleaned and ready to receive company. Their faces are washed and they're happy. Pet them and love them. You'll be proud when someone asks, "How do you keep your irons looking so good?"

# Basic Iron Collecting

# Basic Iron Collecting
## Let's get started

Let's get down to basics. Consider this "Iron Collecting 101." Have you ever wondered how to get started? Don't you wish someone would tell you the tips and tricks? These are the little things that make a big difference. If you are wondering how to begin, relax, help is on the way. Until now, there was no place to find this important basic information. Here it is: simple, basic and to-the-point. You'll discover tried-and-true tips. Even seasoned collectors might be reminded of something long forgotten.

Let's get started.

• An overlooked way to become intimately familiar with irons is to handle them. Visit collections. You'll find a directory of members when you join a club. Take advantage of the opportunity to pick up irons that attract you. There's something about the tactile experience that imprints the mind's memory bank. Hold the iron in your hands. Feel its weight. Is it smooth or rough? How is the balance? Get acquainted. Pet it. Caress it.

As a point of etiquette, it's polite to ask first. This is the same as asking a mother if you may hold the baby. Just say, "May I hold the iron?" Permission is usually freely granted. If not, accept the refusal gracefully.

*To safely lift an iron, keep one hand underneath.*

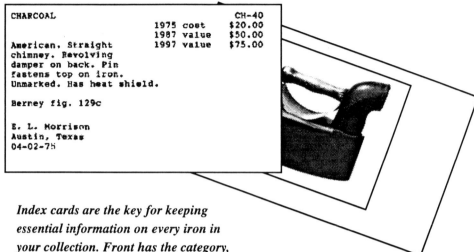

*Index cards are the key for keeping essential information on every iron in your collection. Front has the category, unique file number, purchase price, purchase date, changes in value. Marks, comments and references are recorded as well as the source. A photo is on the reverse.*

One knows to support the infant's head with one hand. It's the same with irons, particularly those with detachable handles. They have been known to separate with disastrous consequences. Lift with one hand and keep the other underneath. If the catch fails, you're still in control.

• Most collectors will be happy for you to see their collections. A knowledgeable collector can be helpful. There's a world of information available if you ask the right questions. Be courteous (your mother told you that) and generous with your compliments. You'll be welcome, especially if you indicate intelligent interest. We hope you won't be guilty of the common mistake—searching through the collection to find examples of irons you already have. Be interested in irons you haven't seen before.

Instead of trying to impress your host with your knowledge, exercise humility and ask questions. Be receptive and open to new facts. You'll be surptised at what you can learn. As you see particular pieces, you'll be inspired to inquire about them. An advanced collector may not be comfortable volunteering information without an indication of what you want to know. Some people aren't receptive to instruction. If this doesn't describe you, encourage the flow of ideas. One good opener is, "What can you tell me about this iron?"

It's your responsibility to guide the conversation in a direction that'll help you the most. You may find some subjects illicit less than frank responses. It's considered gauche to inquire about price or where the iron came from. Some collectors don't mind revealing their sources and amount paid. But it's best to avoid sensitive subjects.

• Keep records. In the beginning, it's easy to remember everything about each piece in your collection. It's hard to discipline yourself, but necessary. Later, you will be glad you did. Details become hazy with time. Make a record. Write it down. Key it into the computer. Here are some of the things you should include:

**Number**
(Assign a unique number for each piece.)
**Kind or category**
(Charcoal, sad, etc.)
**Name**
(Sensible, Eagle, etc.)
**Brief description**
(What makes it different or interesting?)
**Country of origin**
(USA, France, etc.)
**Remarks**
(Anything else you would like to say.)
**Marks**
(Patent dates, manufacturer's name, etc.)
**Price**
(How much did you pay?)
**Source**
(Where did you get it?)
**Acquisition date**
(When did you get it?)
**References**
(Page or figure numbers in books)
**Documentation**
(Invoice, history, etc.)
It's also nice to include a photograph.

*The family hearth is a natural place for prized irons. Find spots in your home where irons fit naturally. Live surrounded by your collection. You and your irons will be happier.*

*Pyramid heaters enhance a collection while offering an interesting display opportunity. Look for these, other heaters and laundry stoves.*

Although this seems elaborate, it's stressed only because you can save a lot of hassle by keeping good records from the start. If you wait until later, your difficulties will be enormous.

• Look for iron heaters and laundry stoves. They make good display stands for your irons. A pyramid heater will accommodate three sad irons in an attractive arrangement. Laundry stoves are designed with racks holding six or more irons around the belly. Additional irons can be displayed on the top.

• Be hungry for information. Find out everything you can about irons. Books are your friends. Beginning collectors often begrudge money spent on books. A familiar excuse is, "For that amount, I could have bought an iron." Books are important because knowledge is power. You'll discover irons you didn't know existed. You'll be inspired. Buy books—and read them. They are worthwhile and you'll be glad you did.

• Subscribe to *IRON TALK*.

• Join an iron club and attend meetings. You'll meet other collectors and make friends who love irons as much as you. Clubs are a good source for information on sales, auctions and international meetings. There's always the opportunity to buy and trade. There are iron collecting clubs in several countries. To join the Midwest Sad Iron Collectors Club, send $20.00 to:

Lynette Conrad
Secretary/Treasurer, MISICC
24 Nob Hill Drive
St. Louis, MO 63138-1458

• Get the best you can afford. Resist the temptation to economize. Avoid broken irons, avoid irons with missing parts, avoid repaired irons, avoid irons in poor condition, avoid excessive rust. Get the best example of the type you are acquiring.

*Books are your friends. Build a personal reference library. Books will increase your knowledge and add credibility to your collection.*

*Go to antique fairs, flea markets, shows and malls. You'll find irons, make friends and build memories for a lifetime.*

Today, irons are mostly purchased. The period of no-cost irons being there for the finding is almost over. Now, nearly every addition to the collection involves a cost. As time passes, you'll find that the value of irons in good condition will increase faster than ones in bad condition. From an investment perspective, it's good business to acquire the best. The superior pieces will consistently provide the satisfaction you expect.

Irons are a commodity. Expect to pay for what you get. If you are thinking about adding one of the rare and beautiful pieces, chances are it will cost more than an average iron. Yes, it will cost more because it is worth more and you'll feel better about it.

*Take care when offered a piece like this. No, it is not a valuable never-before-seen example. This is a shotgun marriage of a Sensible handle and an Ober sleeve iron base. A hole drilled in the heel is fitted with a looping rod to hold the handle. This will never have a collector's value.*

• Look for irons. They won't look for you. Some collectors are becoming discouraged because irons are not as easy to find as they used to be. But irons are still there. You just have to look harder and know where to look. Go out and rustle and hustle. Go where the irons are. You'll be surprised at what you turn up.
• Here's where to find irons:
Flea markets.
Auctions.
Antique shows.
Garage sales.
Antique malls.
Antique publications.
Dealers.
Trade with other collectors.
Nearly every collector has a few duplicates and upgrades for trade.
Ask family and friends.
There're still irons in old basements, barns and attics.
Iron club meetings have trade and sale sessions.

*Irons are where you find them, even in this old barn.*

Irons are out there, waiting for you. On any day of the week, in any major city, you can find an antique iron before noon.
• Look for something you don't have. Don't be satisfied with the easily-found sad irons and detachable handle irons. Promise yourself a different kind of iron to add variety.

*What's wrong with this iron? The Jubilee, with its distinctive protruding burner pipe, is a desirable fuel iron. However, this one is missing the valve wheel and filler cap. These parts could be difficult to replace.*

• Avoid repos. Keep your collection from becoming contaminated. Remember the old adage "One bad apple can spoil the barrel."
• Care for and clean your irons (see "Secrets of Cleaning Irons" *IRON TALK* issue No. 8). Irons look better if they are cleaned and not left in "as found" condition. Some irons haven't been cleaned in a hundred years. They deserve better treatment than that. Is there anything else around your house that has been neglected for a century? Of course not, and the irons should

# 10 Most Frequent Mistakes

**1. Buying irons that are broken or lacking parts.**

Broken irons are an embarrassment and a poor investment. Missing parts are usually even more difficult to find than a complete iron.

**2. Passing up opportunities expecting to find something cheaper.**

When you see something you want, that's the time to get it. Too often, the moment will not present itself again. Every collector has tales of regret—opportunities not taken—offers rejected—chances ignored.

**3. Slow to act.**

There may be long periods with no collecting activity, then there's a flurry of buying and trading. Make the most of circumstances to add to your collection.

**4. Duplicates.**

If you have more than one of a thing, you are not a collector, you are an accumulator.

**5. Buying quantity, not quality.**

You'll be happier with one good thing than with a shelf full of losers.

**6. Afraid to ask questions.**

Nearly every other collector knows something that can help you.

**7. Complaining about market values.**

"Good irons are too hard to find." "Irons are too expensive." "Nothing is the same anymore." That's the way life is. Get over it.

**8. Provincial.**

Don't expect to find everything you want in your backyard. Some collectors rarely look 100 miles beyond their home. Move farther afield. Go to sales in another state. Consider the world as your venue.

**9. Ignoring books.**

Access to printed material is absolutely essential.

**10. Self-centered.**

Your irons are like your children. You love them and and they seem to be the most gorgeous ever made. Restrain the passion for your possessions. Admire the collections of others, learn from them and display modesty.

---

be no exception. Clean your irons. They'll be happier and you'll enjoy them more.

• Think about how to display irons. The worst places are out of sight in an unused cellar or garage. High humidity and changes in temperature are devastating to irons. They belong in the house so you can live among them. And this means someplace other than the laundry room. The beautiful ones will be comfortable in the living room. A mantle or hearth is the natural home of some favorite irons. Put others in a sewing room. They belong everywhere, including the bedrooms. You'll have pleasant dreams if irons are the last thing you see before going to sleep. And don't neglect the guest rooms. Share your enthusiasm with visitors by decorating the spare bedroom with your lovely irons.

Bill and Bente Picken display their travel irons in the guest bedroom, slyly pointing out the apt association of traveling guests with traveling irons.

• Add a special iron to go with the more common pieces that constitute the core collection. Study the literature and allow inspiration to lead you forward. The more you learn, the more there is to learn. You'll never know it all. You'll never have it all. That's the attraction. That's the allure. Enjoy it—go for it—join the fun.

• If you are going to be an iron collector, be an iron collector. Avoid walking down the path into unrelated categories. A person who is focused usually does better than one spread among several disciplines. Be an iron collector first, second and always.

*Umbrellas blossom in the rain at Brimfield. That's Carol Walker with the cart. Do you suppose it's loaded with irons? The lesson of this picture is: be prepared for the weather.*

35

*The sales room at the Midwest Sad Iron Collectors Club offers hundred of irons at reasonable prices. This is a great place to buy irons and talk with other collectors.*

*The "go-with" items, ancillary soaps, washboards and starch boxes, can add color and interest to an iron collection.*

When irons are difficult to find, it's tempting to ease the collecting instinct by being satisfied with something else. This can only result in a mediocre collection. People with multiple interests rarely develop the consuming passion that drives a committed iron collector. If you have never used the food money to buy an iron, you are not a dedicated collector.

• Look for soaps, starch packages, advertising and washboards. These are great to spark up the display, bringing a new dimension to the collection by adding color and interest. This is not an invitation to dilute the iron collection with a hodgepodge of unrelated material. "Go-alongs" intimately relate to the subject of irons. Use them sparingly, not overdoing it, and the result can be extremely positive.

• Let everyone know you are an iron collector. There's no way to predict when a chance remark will result in an iron acquisition. It pays to advertise. Let everyone know that you are more than interested in irons. They are your life, your love, your passion.

• If you find a special iron and it seems a little high in price, get it. Do without something else. You may never find it again.

• Be the best you can be. Always strive to excel and don't settle for second best. Insist that iron collecting is number one. Remember, "good enough" is never good enough.

• Be aggressive. Go looking. You can't expect someone to take you by the hand, leading you around and pointing out irons. When you are hunting Easter eggs, you have to take your basket and find the eggs yourself.

Good hunting!

36

# Advanced Iron Collecting

# Advanced Iron Collecting
## Tips from the pros

Iron collecting is a noble and important activity. Everyone who preserves historical ironing implements is engaged in a hobby with far-reaching implications. History and time move on relentlessly. Each iron saved from the scrap heap today is a gift to future generations. Every collection, small or large, is significant. However, there comes the time when haphazard accumulation is no longer enough. The basic collector yearns for something more. Advanced collecting is an attractive next step. What does it mean? How is it done? Questions are everywhere. Here are some answers.

Even though the difference between basic and advanced collecting isn't always clear-cut, there *is* a difference. It can be recognized in several ways. There's no mistaking a "fire in the belly" attitude that surrounds serious collectors. They're always looking. Their lives are dominated with irons.

*Howell collection.*
*Sara Howell: "Simply having large numbers of irons does not make one an advanced collector. More important is a basic knowledge of irons—how they were used, their approximate value, approximate age, country of origin and how they were made."*

Instead of playing tennis, they're hunting irons. Instead of going fishing, they're attending sales. Every weekend is another iron trip. Their focus remains bright.

Contrary to expectation, the size of a collection isn't the defining factor. The ordinary collection has run-of-the-mill irons. Sara Howell tells of visiting the home of a woman who boasted a collection of over 3,000 irons. "They were everywhere—in heaps on the floor,

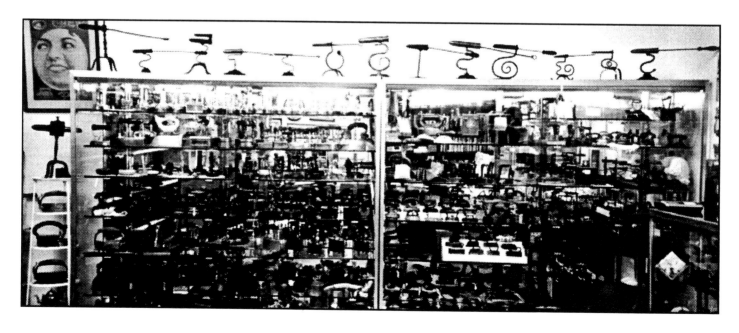

*Walker collection.*
*Carol Walker: "When you find an iron you really want, just open your pocketbook."*

on shelves, on tables and spilling off other furniture. I did not dare to pick up an iron for fear of creating a landslide. I asked her if she had the 'Ne Plus Ultra' and she replied, 'I don't know what that is!' She had thousands of common irons, but no historical knowledge of irons."

Sara concludes, "We have seen small collections that contained rare and beautiful irons."

It isn't the number of irons, but the care and intelligence that makes the difference. It's a rare collector, however, who is satisfied to stop with a certain number. Irons get in the blood. If you have one model, you'll want others by the same manufacturer. Nothing else stirs the acquisitive juices as much as the possibility of getting a fine iron the collector doesn't already own.

A distinguishing characteristic of an advanced collection is the difficulty of assembling it. There'll be rare and unusual pieces. Hard-to-find irons migrate into the hands of the serious collector.

An advanced iron collector is expected to know the basics. What is the country of origin? Learn the difference between American and European irons. Have a knowledge of market prices and learn why some irons command higher valuations than others.

Speak the lingo. An advanced collector knows that a box iron and a slug iron are the same. There's no difference between a charcoal iron and a coal iron. Know what a goffering iron is. Be familiar with the terms "slickenstone" and "polisher." Be able to explain how they were used.

Bruce Baumunk explains that collecting is a learning process. From his own experience, he says, "Once you get past the junk stage, you begin to think about more expensive irons. By the time you realize the good stuff is worth paying for, you've passed up a lot."

The beginning collector is attracted to whatever is available and cheap. This can be a positive interval if one is ambitious for growth. It's a period for building the core collection. Use it for studying and learning. If the basic collection is systematically formed, it'll smooth the transition to advanced collecting. Before investing heavily, one should be exposed to mature collections. Make friends with knowledgeable collectors. Study books, periodicals and search out sources for research.

Gather information on the irons you have, the irons you would like to have and irons in general. Establish files. Keep records of your collection. Keep a file of advertising, patent papers, letters and assorted iron-related information. Save printed instructions shipped with irons, factory specifications, parts lists—these are all things you should accumulate and preserve. When it's time to make the upward leap, a foundation will be in place.

Advanced collectors reach their position via different routes. They have different approaches and viewpoints.

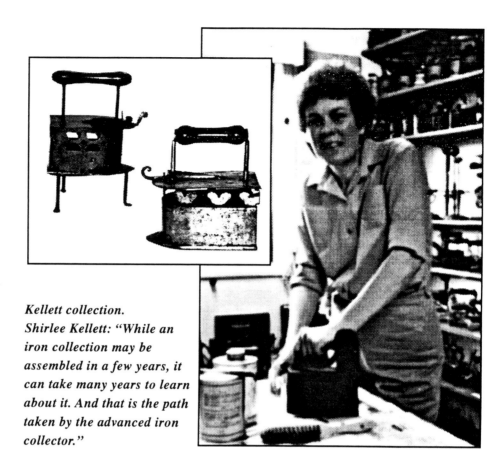

*Kellett collection.*
*Shirlee Kellett: "While an iron collection may be assembled in a few years, it can take many years to learn about it. And that is the path taken by the advanced iron collector."*

*Carson collection.*
*Buck Carson: "You need a strong back and a good memory. It helps to have deep pockets."*

39

*Baumunk collection.*
*Bruce Baumunk: "Once you get past the junk stage, you begin to think about more expensive irons. By the time you realize it is good to pay for the fine stuff, you've passed up a lot.*

Their personalities aren't the same, but most share some characteristics.

Bill Picken knows that top-level iron collectors are more aggressive. He says, "They are avid, dedicated, more knowledgeable and pay more." He illustrates, "I've been known to call my travel agent to book a sudden flight for a weekend. Leaving on a Friday evening, I was back at work Monday after traveling half way across the continent to buy just two irons."

Resolve to be the best you can. Don't accept second best. Stretch to reach beyond your grasp. You'll be surprised at what's possible.

Establish goals. It makes sense to know where you are going. Where do you expect to be in five years? What are you trying to accomplish? Do you want

*Picken collection.*
*Bill Picken: "I've never regretted bringing an iron home, but always feel bad about leaving one behind."*

to assemble a well-selected collection of a broad range of ironing instruments?

Or perhaps you intend to specialize. Before you do this, have an overview of the whole spectrum of iron collecting. In the same way that a specialist doctor is well-versed in all of medicine, so should a specialist in iron collecting know everything possible about the totality of irons. Some collectors are only interested in fluters, little irons or fuel irons. Whatever your interest, focus on your chosen area with a vengeance.

Other goals might be to preserve a part of history or to collect implements illustrating the evolution of ironing. Selecting a goal is a personal experience. Whatever you decide, keep your determination to be the best you can in your selected field. Continue to learn and do research.

Read all you can about irons. A collector unfamiliar with the available literature is at a disadvantage. Study books. Subscribe to *IRON TALK*.

*Irons collection.*
***Dave Irons: "There are still plenty of good irons to be found."***

Two important books by David Irons are *Irons by Irons* and *More Irons by Irons*. These can be ordered directly from the author.

David Irons
223 Covered Bridge Rd.
Northampton, PA 18067
610-262-9335

Visit other collectors. You'll nearly always find an iron you haven't seen before. Collectors are usually generous in sharing information. Don't be afraid to ask about something you don't understand. There are none of us who can't learn something new. Share your knowledge and soak up everything you can learn. Don't expect every iron in an advanced collection to knock your socks off. Mary Balestri explains that all irons are precious. She says, "Just enjoy each iron—whether unusual, rare or common. Give it lots of TLC."

Jerry Wolton speaks from experience: "Study and gaining knowledge is an ongoing process. Some collectors don't bother to educate themselves. You need to at least know the difference between old and new. One must rely on judgment when an iron is not in the books."

Establish an iron network. Have friends who are serious about iron

*Balestri collection.*
***Mary Balestri: "Each person develops his own unique style of collecting over the years depending on interest, time, money, space or for investment."***

    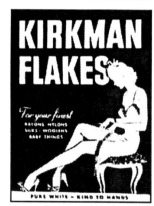

*Walker collection:*
*Carol Walker: "Soap, starch and other laundry products add excitement and interest to an iron collection. The brilliant inks contribute a much needed element of color."*

*Walker collection.*

*Jimmy Walker: "An ancillary collection of laundry products should be displayed sparingly and with restraint, much as seasoning is used in food. It should enhance, not dominate."*

*Wolton collection.*
*Jerry Wolton: "I really like the ones that do something, i.e. fluters, box irons, gas irons and mechanical stuff."*

collectors look for anything they don't have. They accumulate a lot of common stuff. An advanced collector is searching for rare and hard-to-find irons."

"A beginning collector," points out Babe Kinnemeyer, "can find more, but is generally timid and afraid to spend much. The advanced collector, on the other hand, has a much harder task at finding something, but is willing to pay higher prices."

"The difference," according to L. G. Sinclair, "has to do with quality. The advanced collector has more good pieces."

An advanced collector has a greater knowledge of available irons, but is prepared to be surprised when a different one surfaces.

Be aggressive. Keep it light. Keep it friendly. Nobody likes someone who is pushy. Cultivate dealers. Know what you want and go after it. If you just sit around, nothing will happen. Find out where the auctions are. Find out where the sales are. Be there first when the gates open.

collecting. It doesn't matter how far away a collector lives. Develop a long term relationship. Write letters; talk to them on the phone; visit them. Give them a call every so often. Collectors love to talk. You will enjoy chats and always learn something. Know who has what, where it is and what's for sale. This is all part of keeping your focus bright, finding out what you need to know and acting on it.

As your friendships become global, you'll discover that many Europeans favor centuries-old hand-made irons while scorning more recent "industrial-made irons." Other parts of the world appreciate the history and technology represented in manufactured irons. Both groups should be tolerant of each other. Some collections are harmonious mixtures of all types.

Whatever your passion in irons, get the best you can afford. Look for the finest example of the type you are acquiring. Avoid broken irons. Avoid irons with missing parts. Avoid repaired irons. Avoid irons in poor condition. Avoid excessive rust.

Ralph Wiesehan says, "Beginning

*Sinclair/Kohler collection.*
*L. G. Sinclair: "The difference in collectors has to do with quality. The advanced collector has more good pieces."*

Expect to pay for what you get. Irons are a commodity. When you see magnificent irons in a collection, you can assume they didn't get there by accident. Most of them were bought. And the extraordinary examples cost more than common irons.

Hunt them down. If irons light your fire, you don't need any urging. You're already planning vacations to visit iron markets. You're orienting your trips around travel to meetings, sales, shows and opportunities to view important collections.

As an advanced collector, you already know what you like. You have a goal and a plan on how to reach it. It's not the purpose of *IRON TALK* to tell you what kind of irons to get. However, a few general suggestions might be in order.

Keep only one of each iron along with its variations. Don't choke your shelves with duplicates. Don't mix reproductions with genuine irons. Learn to recognize the difference and keep them separate. It's the old story of one bad apple in the barrel. A few repos on a shelf can cast suspicion on all others. In "Basic Iron Collecting" *IRON TALK* Issue No. 14, beginning collectors were cautioned to "avoid repos." This suggestion not to mix them isn't a change of heart, but simply deals with reality. Every collection has a few repos. We know it's going to happen. *IRON TALK* simply asks that you do what's right and segregate them from authentic irons.

Upgrade. When you have the opportunity to get a better example of an iron you already have, count your blessings. Get the better one and sell or trade the original. The difference in cost will probably be minimal. This is how your collection will constantly get better.

Keep excellent records on your irons: where they came from, what they cost, references. Any written record is more permanent and reliable than the best memory.

Look for all versions and variations of a favorite iron. If you collect little irons, for example, get every size and kind of curled handed irons, tri-bumps and swans you can find. There is a special feeling of pride when you look at a line of irons all of one type, yet each different.

*Kinnemeyer collection.*
*Babe Kinnemeyer: "A beginning collector can find more, but is generally timid and afraid to spend much. The advanced collector, on the other hand, has a much harder task at finding something, but is willing to pay higher prices."*

*Wiesehan collection.*
*Ralph Wiesehan: "Beginning collectors look for anything they don't have. An advanced collector is searching for rare and hard-to-find irons."*

*Tonnekreek collection.*
*W.F. v.d. Tonnekreek: "Don't buy too many 'door stops.' Get a knowledge of the subject by talking to other collectors. Don't listen to the 'wisdom' of the fleamarket dealer."*

Some may be critical of the notion of collecting every model and all variations. If you feel this way, you're entitled. But many dedicated collectors justifiably revel in successfully completing a set. This is similar to a coin collector striving to get all coins of a given denomination or year.

Find a place for your collection. As it grows, it gets more unwieldy. Most advanced collectors find a dedicated room for their irons. Your irons are important. Love them and give them shelter.

Look for soaps, starch packages, advertising and washboards. These add a new dimension to the collection, adding color and interest—a splendid way to spark up the display. The "go-withs" can do much to add distinction to a great collection. They shouldn't dominate. Let them be a significant but always secondary part. Other peripheral categories are sprinklers, figurines, candy dishes, butter dishes and iron-related jewelry.

Carry in your mind the vision of a special iron you would like to have. You will be amazed at how effective that mental picture is. The vision can turn wishes into reality. Somehow it works and the iron will come to you. When you have an opportunity for that special iron and it seems a little high in price, get it. Do without something else. You may never find it again.

# IRON TALK'S 1995-1998 Index

## (A)

**Acorn Brass Mfg. Co.**
advertising, No. 9 fig. 2
iron, No. 9 fig. 2
price, No. 9 fig. 60, No. 15 fig. 46
**acorn rear tank iron**
photo, No.9 fig. 14
**Adams, F.C.,** No. 12 p. 2
**"Advanced Iron Collecting,"** No. 15 p. 4
**advertising**
Acorn Brass Mfg. Co., No. 9 fig. 2
Akron Lamp & Mfg. Co., No. 9 fig. 27
American Beauty, No. 5 p. 12 figs. 78-79
Brown Mfg. Co., No. 9 p. 4
"Burns air," No. 9 fig. 26
Clothes Sprinkler, No. 10 fig. 3
"Diamond, The," No. 9 fig. 27
Foote Mfg. Co., No. 9 fig. 10
Household Sprayers, No. 10 fig. 7
"Improved Easy Iron, The," No. 9 fig. 10
Perfecto Sad Iron Factory, No. 9 fig. 19
"Standard" iron, No. 9 p. 4
**advertising iron**
paperweight
Charles Cockshutt & Co.
price, No. 15 fig. 28
Reid Brothers-At the Sign of Red Goose
price, No. 15 fig. 29
**agitator sprinkler**
No. 18 fig. 43
**Akron Lamp Co.**
Montgomery Ward, No.9 fig. 20
**Alba Split chimney charcoal iron**
No. 16 fig. 29
**alcohol iron,** *see* fuel iron, alcohol and named irons
**"Alcomtic"**
price, No. 8 fig. 38
**"All British Pumpless Iron,"**
photo, No. 9 fig. 14
price, No. 9 fig. 35
**Allhands, Jane**
letter, No. 9 fig. 2
*Alte Bygelgeräte*
No. 7 p. 4

**American Model No. 6664**
photo, No. 9 fig. 21
**America,** *see* United States
**American No. 66**
price, No. 9 fig. 38
**American Beauty Iron**
No. 5 p. 12 fig. 80, No. 14 fig. 23
price, No. 5 fig. 60, No. 7 fig. 34, No. 14 fig. 61
**"American Fluting Irons"**
No. 5 p. 5
**American Gas Machine Co.**
No. 16 p. 5
modified triangle tank, No. 9 fig. 21
price, No. 9 fig. 37, No. 13 fig. 38
side tank,
No. 9 fig. 1
No. 16 fig. 9
price, No. 9 fig. 36, No. 13 fig. 37,
No. 16 fig. 38
**American Machine Co.**
crank fluter
price, No. 16 fig. 31
hand rolling fluter
photo, No. 14 fig. 29
price, No. 14 fig. 67
**AMIFER Library**
No. 20 p. 14
**Amish,** No. 12 p. 4
**Anabaptist,** No. 12 p. 4
**"Anatomy of a Fuel Iron,"** No. 9 p. 12
**Anderson, Ian**
"Apprentice's Test Piece, The," No. 13 p. 4
photo, No. 13 p. 4, 7
**Antiques of a Mechanical Nature**
No. 7 p. 8 fig. 25
**Antiques of Essence**
No. 7 p. 8 fig. 25
**Armstrong, Lou Ann**
letter, No. 8 p. 2
**art history**
No. 5 p. 1
**Asbestos boxed set**
No. 4 p. 7

**Asbestos Sad Iron,** No. 14 fig. 21
    price, No. 14 fig. 57
**Asbestos Sleeve Iron**
    price, No. 15 fig. 57
**Atkinson, George and Fran**
    letter, No. 12 p. 2, No. 15 p. 2
**Atkins Patent hot water iron**
    No. 6 p. 8 fig. 22
    price, No. 12 fig. 119
**Atlantic City**
    *See* "Atlantique City," No. 7 p. 7
**auction**
    "Canadian Iron Auction," No. 4 p. 6
**Aunt Sally's**
    No. 5 p. 9

## (B)

**"Baby Betsy Ross"**
    No. 6 p. 5 fig. 10
    price, No. 6 fig. 37
**Balestri, Mary**
    letter, No. 18 p. 2
    No. 15 p. 7, fig 8
**band block**
    price, No. 12 fig. 109
**band block stretcher**
    price, No. 12 fig. 110
**bank**
    Flatiron building, No. 20 fig. 11-14
        price, No. 20 fig. 36-39
**Barclay, Rod**
    letter, No. 11 p. 2
**"Basic Iron Collecting,"** No. 14 p. 4
**Baumunk, Bruce**
    No. 15 p. 5, fig. 6
    letter, No. 16 p. 2
**Baumunk, Charlotte**
    No. 4 p. 6 fig. 15
**Bayart, Achille,** No. 10 p. 12
**Beetall Gas Iron**
    price, No. 19 fig. 46
**Beatrice's Shop,** No. 1 p. 6-7, fig. 19
**Belgian irons**
    w/trivet
        price, No. 19 fig. 71
**Bell, Alexander Graham**
    No. 4 p. 1
**Bennett, Larry**
    letter, No. 19 p. 2
**bentwood handle**
    price, No. 8 fig. 31
**"Beer Can" sprinkler**
    No. 18 fig. 13
    price, No. 18 fig. 47

**Berman, Charles**
    letter, No. 19 p. 2
**Berney, Esther**
    *Pressing Irons and Trivets*
        price
            No. 20, fig. 41
**"Betsy Ross EZ Way"**
    No. 6 p. 3 fig. 4
    price, No. 6 p. 11 fig. 47
**Best, The, hand rocking fluter**
    photo, No. 14 fig. 28
        price, No. 14 fig. 66
**"Best Yet" iron**
    patent paper, No. 9 fig. 13
    photo, No. 9 fig. 13
    price, No. 9 fig. 39
**Best Yet Mfg. Co.,** No. 9 fig. 13
**billiard iron**
    price, No. 16 fig. 18
**Bless and Drake**
    sleeve iron
        No.12 p. 2, No. 14 fig. 42
            price, No. 14 fig. 84
**block,** No. 12 fig. 7
**block creaser,** No. 12, p. 8 fig. 25
**block press,** No. 5 p. 7, 10 fig. 32, 40-43
**blue delft sprinkler,** No. 18 fig. 16
    price, No. 18 fig. 65
**Boberg, Freddie,** No. 13 p. 3
**"Bolta Sprinkler, The," plastic**
    No. 18 fig. 43
**book,** *see* named book
**Borsch, Bob**
    letter, No.9 p. 2, No. 12 p. 2
    letter, No. 19 p. 2
**Botel, Ruth**
    letter, No. 10 p. 2, No. 12 p. 2
**bottom board,** No. 12 p.5, fig. 9
**"Boudoir Iron"**
    price, No. 4 p. 7
**box iron**
    No. 1 p. 1, No. 2 p. 1-5, 10-12, fig. 1-16, 33, No. 3 p. 12 fig. 69, No. 4 p. 7 fig. 14, 17, No. 6 fig. 27, No. 13 p. 4-9, 13, fig. 1-11, 22-25, No. 14 fig. 43, No. 15 over & fig. 1
    cold nose
        price, No. 16 fig. 22
    roundheel
        No. 4 fig. 17, No. 19 fig. 33
    price
        No. 2 fig. 35-50, No. 3 fig. 27, 69, No. 4 p 7 fig. 24-26, No. 5 fig. 46-48, No. 8 fig. 57-58, No. 14 fig. 52, No. 15 fig. 31, No. 16 fig. 19-22
**Boxed set**
    Enterprise with 5 bases, No. 11 fig. 5

48

**Boy and Girl cleanser dispensers,**
   Cleminsons
      No. 10 fig. 4
      price, No. 10 fig. 39
**"Boy" sprinkler, black, new**
   No. 10 fig. 9
   price, No. 10 fig. 52
**Bracht, Alexander**
   letter, No. 12 p. 2
**Brathwaite, Dollie**
   letter, No. 13 p. 2
**Brimfield**
   No. 8 p. 9
**brim iron**
   price, No. 12 fig. 111-113
**Brittany, French charcoal**
   No. 1 p. 3, fig. 7, 25
   price, No. 10 fig. 34-36
**Brown Mfg. Co.**
   advertisement, No. 9 p. 4
**'B. S. & R." polisher**
   price, No. 4 p. 7
**"Budapest"**
   No. 7 fig. 10
   price, No. 7 fig. 43
**"Bud Vase Laundry Damp'ner," plastic**
   No. 18 fig. 43
**"Bugolette Iron"**
   price, No. 7 fig. 43
**Buffalo Toy and Tool toy mangle**
   price, No. 4 p. 7
**bulb (glass) sprinkler**
   No. 18 fig. 8-11
   price, No. 18 fig. 63-64, 74
**bulb (rubber) sprinkler**
   No. 18 fig. 14
**Burdick, Lyona**
   No. 3 p. 5
**Burgess, Robert**
   No. 6 p. 2
**Burres, Sheri**
   No. 18 p. 3
**Bushnell, Carolynn S.**
   letter, No. 10 p 2

## (C)

**Café du Monde,** No. 5 p. 9
**Camion Frères**
   polisher
      price, No. 15 fig. 52
**"Canadian Iron Auction,"** No. 4 p. 6
**"Candy Containers"**
   No. 5 p. 7

electric iron, No. 5 p. 7, fig. 30
   price, No. 5 fig. 49, No. 7 fig. 30
flat iron, No. 5 p. 7 fig. 28
   price, No. 5 fig. 50, No. 7 fig. 29
Olaf Larson tin, No. 5 p. 7 fig. 29
   price, No. 5 fig. 51
ox tongue, No. 5 p. 7 fig. 31
   price, No. 5 fig. 53
Roundtree tin, No. 5 p. 7 fig. 30
   price, No. 5 fig. 52
**cap irons**
   No. 3 p. 8 fig. 23
   price, No. 3 fig. 36, No. 20 fig. 42
**Carroll, Valerie**
   letter, No. 16 p. 2
**Carver, Horace Peck**
   No. 4 p. 3
      patent papers, No. 4 p 2 fig. 2
      "Ladies Friend," No. 4 p. 2-3 fig. 4
         price, No. 4 fig. 53
**Carson, Buck**
   No. 15 fig. 4
**"Category Codes for Iron Collectors"**
   No. 16 p. 9
**Cather, Donna**
   Letter, No. 20 p. 2
**"Cat with Marble Eyes" sprinkler**
   No. 18 fig. 31
   price, No. 18 fig. 48
**Centennial heater**
   price, No. 16 fig. 46
**Central Grocery Company,** No. 5 p. 9
**Ch. Andre & Cie,** No. 7 p. 4
**Chalfant gas jet iron**
   price, No. 12 fig. 118
**Chalfant Manufacturing Co.**
   No. 6 fig. 1
**Chalfant travel irons**
   No. 6 p. 1 fig 1
      price, No. 6 fig. 35-36
**"Champion, The,"** No. 8 fig. 13
   price, No. 8 fig. 56
**charcoal iron**
   No. 1 p. 10 fig. 23, No. 6 p. 8-9 fig. 24, 31A, No 8 fig.
   18, No. 14 fig. 5, 41
      price, No. 4 p. 7, No. 5 fig. 54-58, No. 8 fig. 28-29,
      No. 13 fig. 32, No. 14 fig. 54, 53, No. 15 fig. 32-35,
      No. 16 fig. 23-29
   advertisements
      Priestley & Co., No. 1 p. 12
   "Anatomy of a Charcoal Iron"
      No. 1 p. 12
   "Charcoal Irons" cover story
      No. 1 p. 1
   "Glowing Fuel Iron, The"

No. 20 p. 14
India
massive brass, decorated
No. 19 fig. 31
Netherlands
No. 19 fig. 36
*see also,* named iron
**charcoal iron grate,** No. 1 p. 3, 4, fig. 10
**charm**
Geneva fluter
price, No. 20 fig. 45
**"Carrie Nation" bottle,** No. 10 p. 5 fig. 10
price, No. 10 fig. 32
**"Casey, J. F. & Co.,"** No. 9 fig. 17
price, No. 9 fig. 46
**"Casper" sprinkler**
letter, No. 18 fig. 4
**cav iron**
price, No. 12 fig. 114
**Chalfant "Toilet Smoothing Iron"**
No. 6 fig. 1
price, No. 6 fig. 35-36
**charcoal irons**
*see also,* named irons
**Chartres Street,** No. 5 p. 8
**Chattanooga iron**
price, No. 19 fig. 74
**Chinaman**
"Cholly"
No. 18 fig. 38
price, No. 18 fig. 52
"Emperor"
No. 18 fig. 40
price, No. 18 fig. 49
"...Holding an Iron"
No. 18 fig. 37
price, No. 18 fig. 50
"...Holding a Towel"
No. 18 fig. 42
"...with removable head"
No. 18 fig. 36
price, No. 18 fig. 51
**Chinese sprinkler,** *see* Chinaman sprinkler
**chrome cleaning,** No. 8 p. 5
**Clark hand fluter**
No. 5 p. 5 fig. 19
price, No. 5 fig. 58, No. 7 fig. 32
**Classen patent,** No. 5 p. 7 fig. 26
price, No. 5 fig. 58, No 7 fig. 32
**classification**
No. 3 p. 1, 6
*See Tuesday's Children*
**cleaning irons**
reader's letter, No. 8 p. 2
"Secrets of Cleaning Irons," cover story

No. 8 p. 1
**cleanser dispensers**
cover story, "Not Quite Sprinklers,"
No. 10 p. 1
*see also,* named dispensers
**Clospray plastic sprinkler**
No. 18 fig. 44
**clothespin sprinkler**
No. 18 fig. 2, 4
price, No. 18 fig. 55
**clothespin sprinkler, plastic**
No. 18 fig. 3
**clothes sprayer,** *see* sprayer, clothes
**"Clothes Sprinkers"**
cover story, No. 18 p. 4
**club, iron collecting**
Midwest Sad Iron Collectors Club
No. 20 p. 2
**Colebrookdale,** No. 14 fig. 20
**Cole, Henrietta,** No. 5 p. 5
**Cole crank fluter,** No. 5 p. 5-6 fig. 21
price, No. 5 fig. 61, No. 7 fig. 36
**Coleman Company, Inc.**
"Early Coleman Irons," cover story
No. 16 p. 4
**Coleman iron**
advertisement
No. 16 fig. 26
No. 8 fig. 10
"Early Coleman Irons," cover story
No. 16 p. 4
Model No. 1
No. 16 p. 12, 14, fig. 1, 2, 22, 23, 25
Model No. 2
No. 16, p. 15, fig. 1, 2, 24, 25, 26
price, No. 15 fig. 45
Model No. 4
price, No. 15 fig. 44
Model No. 4-A
No. 1 fig. 53
No. 2 fig. 60
No. 14 p. 9 fig. 15-17
price, No. 8 fig. 41, No. 13 fig. 40,
No. 14 fig. 69
Model No. 5
No. 9 fig. 18
price, No. 9 fig. 41
Model No. 12
No. 13, p. 2
price, No. 13 fig. 39
Model No. 615
No. 9 fig. 22
price, No. 9 fig. 41, No. 16 fig. 39
Model No. 614A
No. 2 fig. 29, 59

Museum
No. 16 p. 5, fig. 3
post WWII models
No. 20 p. 2
production dates
Toronto, Canada
No. 20 p. 2
Wichita, KS USA
No. 20 p. 2
**collecting**
iron
"Advanced Iron Collecting," No. 15 p. 4
"Basic Iron Collecting, " No. 14 p. 4
changing, No. 7 p. 8
**collections**
Balestri, Mary No. 15 fig. 8
Baumunk,Bruce No. 15 fig. 6
Collins, Betty, No. 4 p. 6 fig. 15
Carson, Buck No. 15 fig. 4
Howell, Sara No. 15 fig. 3
Irons, Dave No. 15 fig. 9
Kellett, Shirlee No. 15 fig. 5
Kinnemeyer, Babe, No. 15 fig. 14
Picken, Bill, No. 15 fig. 7
Sinclair/Kohler, No. 15 fig. 13
Walker, Carol and Jimmy No. 15 fig. 2,
10-11
Wiesehan, Ralph, No. 15 fig. 15
Wolton, Jerry No. 15 fig. 12
*see also,* Collectors
**Collectors**
"Evans, Eloise," No. 2 p. 8-9 fig. 26-32
Irons, Dave "More Irons by Irons," No. 8 p. 7
fig. 13-21
"Payne, Pete and Nancy," No. 6 p. 8 fig. 21-32
"Picken, Bente and Bill," No. 19 p. 8 fig. 26-40
***Collector's Guide to Trivets & Stands, The***
letter from Larry Bennett, No. 19 p. 2
**combination iron**
box iron/fluter
*see* Streeter patent
charcoal/fluter
*see* Classen patent
electric
*see* travel irons
reversible
cover story "Reversible Combination
Irons, No. 4 p. 1
*see* Fox, Henry C. iron
*see* "King Iron, The"
*see* Mann, A. S.
*see* Young, Hewitt & Mooney
sad/fluter
No. 4 p. 8
*see* Knapp patent

**Colt gas iron,** No. 14 fig. 36
price, No. 14 fig. 76
**Commander's Palace,** No. 5 p. 8
**Cook, Mary Ann B., polisher**
price, No. 8 p. 3
**cookstove, pressed glass**
No. 2 p. 6-7, fig. 17-19, 25, 61-62
**cookware, cast iron**
cleaning, No. 8 p. 3
**cooler, iron,** No. 14 fig. 14, p. 14 fig. 48-51
price, No. 14 fig. 56
**combination**
fluter/sad
Anderson, Charles
price, No. 1 fig. 50, No. 2 fig. 55
No. 15 fig. 38
Myers goat fluter
No. 15 fig. 1
price, No. 15 fig. 39
reversible
*see also* named iron
**commander,** No. 12 p. 6, fig. 10
**computer**
No. 16 p. 7
**comic valentine,** No. 9 fig. 28, p. 10 fig. 33, 34
**cone for hat-body former,** No. 12 p. 14
**"Core Collection, The,"** No. 14 p. 10
**cover stories**
"Advanced Iron Collecting," No. 15 p. 4
"Apprentice's Test Piece, The," No. 13 p. 4
"Basic Iron Collecting," No. 14 p. 4
"Charcoal Irons," No. 1 p. 1
"Clothes Sprinklers," No. 18 p. 4
"Early Coleman Irons," No. 16 p. 4
"Flatiorn Building Collectibles," No. 20 p. 4
"Little Swan Irons," No. 19 p. 4
"Mrs. Florence Potts: The True Story"
No. 11 p. 1
"19th Century Hatter," No. 12 p. 4
"Not Quite Sprinklers" No. 10 p. 1
"Record Keeping for Iron Collectors"
No. 16 p. 4
"Tailgates" No. 2 p. 8
"Tanks for the Memories" No. 9 p. 1
**Cracker Jack prize,** No. 3 p. 12 fig. 62
**crimper**
No. 7 p. 1 fig. 3-4
price, No. 7 figf. 52-53
**Croft, Wilbur and Co.,** No. 5 p. 7
**cross hatch iron**
No. 3 p. 2 fig. 4A
**cross rib iron**
No. 3 p. 2 fig. 3
price, No. 3 fig. 29, No. 4 fig. 34, No. 5 fig. 69

51

**Crown crank fluter**
    No. 14 fig. 39
        price, No. 4 p. 7, No. 14 fig. 65, No. 16 fig. 32
**crown creaser**
    price, No. 12 fig. 115
**crown iron,** No. 12 p. 10, fig. 29, 30
    price, No. 12 fig. 116
**Cummings,** *see* Taliaferro & Cummings
**curled handle iron**
    No. 3 p. 1 fig. 2
    price, No. 3 fig. 30-31, No. 4 fig. 35-36
    *See also,* litte, curled handle
**cylinder grip iron**
    No. 3 p. 2 fig. 5
    price, No. 3 fig. 32-33

## (D)

**"Dalli" charcoal iron**
    No. 1 fig. 29, No. 20 fig. 27
    price, No. 16 fig. 27, No. 20 fig. 43
    advertisement
        No. 20 fig. 26
**"Dallinette"**
    advertisement
        No. 20 fig. 26
**Dann, Herbert Jr.**
    letter, No. 16 p. 2
**Davis, Bill**
    letter, No. 16 p. 2
**Davis, Bob**
    letter, No. 5 p. 2, No. 13 p. 2
**Davis, Jean and Don**
    letter, No. 11 p.2
**"Dearie is Weary" sprinkler**
    No. 10 fig. 2, No. 18 fig. 29
    price, No. 10 fig. 49, No. 18 fig. 56
**Deco irons,** No. 13 fig. 15
**detachable handle iron**
    Enterprise and others, No. 1 fig. 5,
    No. 2 fig. 56
    price, No. 13 fig. 34, 35
    *See also,* named iron
**detachable handle iron, little**
    *See* Enterprise Centennial
**Deutsche Continental Gas Geselschaft**
    No. 7 p. 4
**"Diamond, The," iron,** No. 9 fig. 27
    No. 14 fig. 22
    gasoline or kerosene?, No. 9 p. 12
    price, No. 4 p. 7, No. 9 fig. 42, No. 13 fig. 49, No. 14
    fig. 70
**diamond grip iron**
    price, No. 4 p. 7
**"Dion" hand fluter**
    No. 16 fig. 27

**Di Martino, Vittorio**
    letter, No. 12 p.2
**Dinner, Craig**
    letter, No. 18 p. 2
**directions, fluting**
    No. 4 p. 8-9
**dishes, glass (iron and stove shaped)**
    No. 7 p. 2
**dispenser, cleanser,** *see* named dispenser
**documentation file**
    No. 16 p. 7
**doll house box iron**
    No. 3 p. 12 fig. 65
**Donovan, John C.,** No.8 p. 2
**D'Orsay curling machine**
    price, No. 12 fig. 117
**"Doty" fluter**
    No. 5 p. 5 fig. 18
    price, No. 5 p. 11 fig. 67, No. 7 fig. 41
**Doucette, Paul and Patrice**
    letters, No. 5 p. 2, No. 14 p. 2, No 20 p. 2
**"Dover" store display**
    price, No. 4 p. 7
**"Dover" toy**
    902
        price, No.4 p. 7
    "Dolly"
        price, No. 4 p. 7
**dragon chimney iron**
    No. 8 fig. 18
    price, No. 8 fig. 29
**"Drenth" iron,** No. 1 p. 2
**duck iron,** *see* swan
**"Dudley" crank fluter**
    No. 5 p. 5 fig. 20, No. 16 fig. 33
    price, No. 5 p. 11 fig. 62
**Dunne, Patrick,** No. 5 p. 8
**Durham, Mark F.,** No. 5 p. 5-7
**"Dutch Boy" sprinkler,** No. 10 fig. 16. No. 18 fig. 26
    price, No. 10 fig. 54, No. 18 fig. 57
**Dutch charcoal iron**
    decorator
        letterfrom Jean Serva, No. 16 p. 2
**"Dutch Girl" plastic sprinkler**
    No. 18 fig. 43
**"Dutch Girl" wetter-downer,** No. 10 fig. 16,
    No. 18 fig. 26
    price, No. 10 fig. 65, No. 18 fig. 58
**Dutch stand,** No. 1 p. 2

## (E)

**"Eagle" crank fluter**
    No. 7 p. 3
    price, No. 7 fig. 35

"Eagle" crank fluter, little
No. 7 p. 3 fig. 6-7
price, No. 7 fig. 54-55
early fuel iron
photo, No. 9 fig. 15
price, No. 9 fig. 43
"Economist, The" reversible combination
price, No. 15 fig. 36
Ebendorf, Herb
No. 16 p. 3, 5-6, fig. 4, 7
letter, No. 7 p. 2,
Eckmann, Estherlea "Lee"
letter, No. 16 p. 2
Eckstein, Janet
letter, No. 12 p. 2
letter, No. 13 p. 2
"Economist, The"
No. 4 p. 3
edge iron, No. 12 p. 7, fig. 17
Edison, Thomas Alva, No. 4 p. 1
egg iron
price, No. 20 fig. 47
electric
price, No. 20 fig. 48
"Egyptian Sprinkler"
No. 18 fig. 12
price, No. 18 fig. 59
electric irons
first patent, No. 16 p. 2
Deco
other
No. 14 fig. 23
price, No. 14 fig. 61-63
working order, value of, No. 9 p. 2
see also, named iron
electric iron invention, No. 16 p. 2
electric light invention, No. 4 p. 1
electric style little iron
No. 3 p. 12 fig. 64
"elephant" sprinkler
No. 18 fig. 35
price, No. 18 fig. 60
"elephant, fat" sprinkler
No. 18 fig. 34
price, No. 18 fig. 61
"Elite, The"
No. 6 p. 5 fig. 9A
price, No. 6 p.11 fig. 67
Ellwood, Jim
No. 7 p. 7 fig. 22
English little iron
No. 3 p. 12 fig. 65
Enterprise iron
"Centennial"
No. 3 p. 12 fig. 66

price, No. 3 p. 11 fig. 34, No. 5 fig. 70
"Star Polisher"
price, No. 4 p. 7
Enterprise Manufacturing Company
No. 11, fig. 1, 3
Enterprise Tool and Metal Works
No. 9 p. 6
No. 16 p. 9-11, fig. 13-15
Enterprise trade cards
"Mrs. Potts Advertising Trade Cards"
No. 11 p. 5, fig. 6-96
Enterprise polisher, No. 14 fig. 45
price, No. 14 fig. 77
ephemera, No. 5 p. 4
Etna, No. 7 p. 6
Evans
Eloise
No. 2 p. 8-9, fig. 26-32
letter, No. 5 p. 2
Kristopher
letter, No. 14 p. 2
Norman
No. 2 p. 8, fig. 26
"Ever Ready" stand, No. 1 p. 2
*Evolution of the Sad Iron, The*
No. 3 p. 6, No. 16 p. 12
price, No. 20 fig. 40
E-Z Iron, The
No. 16 p. 9-11, fig. 13-16

(F)

Fairbrother, Roger
letter, No. 5 p. 2
drawing by, No. 13 fig. 2
Falkirk Iron Company
catalog No. 123, No. 13 fig. 11
"Family Laundry Iron"
No. 4 p. 3 fig. 5
price, No. 4 fig. 50
"Farmer and Wife" sprinkler
No. 18 fig. 17
price, No. 18 fig. 66
"Faultless, The"
No. 16 p. 12
Featured Iron
"American Beauty," No. 5 p. 12 fig. 78-80
"Brittany Charcoal," No. 10 p. 12 fig. 66-69
"Coleman Iron 4A," No. 14 p. 9 fig. 15-17
"Crown Iron," No. 12 p. 9 fig. 29-30
"English Cap Iron," No. 3 p. 8 fig. 23
"Hotpoint Utility Iron," No. 6 p. 12 fig. 69-71
"King Iron, The," No. 4 p. 8-9 fig. 20-21
"Linen Press," No. 8 p. 12 fig. 59-61
"Porcelain handle," No. 2 p. 12, fig. 68-69
"Rocking Gas Heater," No. 7 p. 12, fig.64-66

53

"Scottish Box Iron," No. 13 p. 13 fig. 22-25
"Viking Horse," No. 15 p. 13, fig. 18-23
"Vulkan," No. 1 p. 2
"Wonder Iron, The," No. 9 p. 9 fig. 29
**Feldmeyer,** fuel, alcohol
No. 6 p. 6
price, No. 6 fig. 44, No. 16 fig. 37
**figure numbers,** No. 6 p. 2
**figurine**
Chinese tailor
price, No. 20 fig. 51
"Girl Ironing"
price, No. 20 fig. 50
"Girl with Iron" Lladro
price, No. 20 fig. 52
"Flat Iron Girl" bronze
price, No. 20 fig. 49
**Fingerman**
Arlene, No. 4 p. 5 fig. 13
Jerry, No. 4 p. 5 fig. 13, No. 7 p. 2
**Fingerman collection**
No. 20 fig. 21, 22
**"Fingerman's Collection on TV,"** No. 4 p. 5
**Fink, Howard**
letter, No. 16 p. 2
**Finn, George**
patent, No. 1 p. 2
**"Fireman, The" sprinkler**
No. 18 cover fig. 1
price, No. 18 fig. 62
**flange,** No. 12 p. 7, fig. 20, 21
**flange stand,** No. 12 p. 7, fig. 20, 21
**Flatiron building**
cover story,"Flatiorn Building Collectibles," No. 20 p. 4, fig. 1-22
location
address, No. 20 fig. 2
description of site, No. 20 fig. 1
**flat iron,** No. 5 p. 8 fig. 35
price, No. 5 p. 8 fig. 75-77
**Flat Iron Girl**
bronze, No. 20 fig. 5
postcards, No. 20 fig. 4
**"Florida" sprinkler**
No. 18 fig. 18
price, No. 18 fig. 67
**"Flott" iron**
bag of fuel, No. 20 fig. 24
**flower iron,** No. 14 fig. 44
price, No. 14 fig. 64
**fluter, crank,** *see* named fluter
**fluting fork**
No. 14 fig. 26, No. 16 p. 8 fig. 9, p. 11 fig. 10
price, No. 14 fig. 68
**fluter, hand**

*See* block press
*See also* named fluter
**fluter, little**
"Little Fluters" cover story, No. 7 p. 1, 3 fig. 1-7
tinier, No. 7 p. 1 fig. 1
price, No. 7 fig. 57
tiny, No 7 p. 1 fig. 1
price, No. 7 fig. 58
**fluting directions,** No. 4 p. 8-9
**fluting machines historical period**
No. 4 p. 1
**font**
discussion of terms, No. 9 p. 1, 12
*See also* tank
**Foote Mfg. Co.**
advertisement, No. 9 fig. 10
**foot tolliker,** No. 8 p. 6, 10 fig. 11, 22-24
**fluting fork,** No. 16 fig. 9, p. 11 fig. 10
**foundry**
pouring metal, Fig. 13 fig. 28
**fount**
discussion of terms, No. 9 p. 1, 12
*See also* tank
**Fox, Henry C.** iron, No. 4 p. 1 fig. 1-2
price, No. 4 fig. 51
**Fox Sad-Iron Company,** No. 4 p. 3
**freeform tank iron**
photo, No. 9 fig. 16
**French Quarter,** No. 5 p. 8-9
**French Quarter Candy Market,** No. 5 p. 9
**French irons**
little, No. 3 p. 4 fig. 15
price, No. 3 fig. 37, No. 5 fig. 71
L. Tillet No. 3
price, No. 19 fig. 72
porcelain
price, No. 19 fig. 73
**Frigidaire washer agitator sprinkler**
No. 18 fig. 43
**fuel**
briquetts
Chemical Radium Fuel, No. 1 p. 1
Glühstoff fuel, No. 1 p. 5
**fuel iron, alcohol**
No. 6 p. 2, 5-6 fig. 3, 11-13
*See also* named irons
**fuel iron, petroleum**
"Anatomy of a Fuel Iron," No. 9 p. 12
benefits
No. 9 p. 6
cover story
"Tanks for the Memories" No. 9 p. 1
dangers
No. 9 p. 6
early

photo, No. 9 fig. 15
gasoline or kerosene? No. 9 p. 12
working principle, No. 9 p. 12
*See also* named irons
**Fuhrmann, Sherry**
letter, No. 19 p. 2
**Fuluse Iron,** No. 6 p. 3 fig. 7
price, No. 6 fig. 48

## (G)

**Gad-A-Bout K-M iron**
price, No. 6 fig. 49
**"Gallery of Little Swan Irons"**
No. 19. p. 6, fig. 10-25
**Garrett, Duane**
letter, No. 8 p. 2
**gasoline iron,** *see* fuel iron, petroleum
**gas iron**
No. 7 p. 4 fig. 8-19
price, No. 7 fig. 42-49, No. 8 fig. 48-49
*See also* named iron
**"Gem" gas iron**
No. 6 p. 5 fig. 9B
price, No. 6 fig. 40, No. 15 fig. 61
**"Gem" polisher**
price, No. 8 fig. 50
**"Gemo" charcoal iron**
price, No. 16 fig. 26
**Geneva fluter charm**
price, No. 20 fig. 45
**"Geneva hand fluter"**
No. 1 fig. 52, No. 2 fig. 57, No. 5 p. 5 fig. 17, No. 7
p. 1, No. 14 fig. 19
price, No. 6 fig. 40, No. 13 fig. 36
**"Geneva hand fluter," little**
No. 7 p. 1 fig. 2
price, No. 7 fig. 56
**"Geneva Improved hand fluter"**
price, No. 16 fig. 35
**Geneva tailor iron**
No. 14 fig. 24
price, No. 14 fig. 85
**Gerds, Gale,** No. 10 p. 4
**G. E. travel iron**
price, No. 4 p. 7
**Gillis, Richard,** No. 7 p. 2
**"Girl" sprinkler, black, new,** No. 10 fig. 9, 18
price, No. 10 fig. 53
**"Girl with Doll," sprinkler,** No. 10 fig. 2
price, No. 10 fig. 55
**glass**
*see* Cookstove, pressed glass
*see* sad iron, pressed glass
**glass dishes (iron and stove shaped)**
No. 7 p. 2

**glass sad iron**
Sun Flame, price No. 19 fig. 49
**glass sprinkler**
No. 18 fig. 8-12
price, No. 18 fig. 59, 63-64, 74
**Glissman, A. H.**
No. 3 p. 6, No. 16, p. 3
**Glissman, Edna**
No. 3 p. 6, No. 16, p. 3
*The Evolution of the Sad Iron*
price, No. 20 fig. 40
**"Glossary, Hatters',"** No. 12 p. 10
**"Glowing Fuel Iron, The"**
No. 20 p. 14
**"Goebel" elephant decanter**
No. 10 p. 5 fig. 12
price, No. 10 fig. 40
**goffering iron**
group of five, No. 19 fig. 40
monkey tail, No. 8 fig. 15, No. 19 fig. 40
price, No 8 fig. 41
three barrels, No. 4 p. 6 fig. 14, No. 15, cover and
fig. 1
price, No. 4 p. 7
No. 19 fig. 40
two barrels, No. 19 fig. 40
serpent upright
No. 19 fig. 40
price, No. 19 fig. 50
**goffering machine,** No. 10, fig. 28, p. 10
fig. 29-31
**goffering pin**
No. 2 p. 5, 10, fig. 16, 33-34
No. 1 p. 3-4, fig. 10
**goffering stack**
price, No. 16 fig. 45
**Gothamware plastic sprinkler**
No. 18 fig. 45
**Greenwood, Ray**
letter, No. 19 p. 2
**Graybar**
photo, No. 14 fig. 51
price, No. 14 fig. 62
**Grand Union Tea Company,** No.12 p. 2
**grate, charcoal iron,** No. 1 p. 3, 4, fig. 10
**green ivy sprinker,** No. 18 fig. 16
price, No. 18 fig. 65
**Green, Karen**
letter, No. 18 p. 2
**Green, Tommy**
No. 18 p. 3
**Griswold**
set of three bases, No. 8 fig. 32
**Grossman. Bob**
address: No. 11 p. 11

55

"Mrs. Potts Advertising Trade Cards"
No. 11 p. 5
**Gulbrandsen, Anniken**
letter, No. 15 p. 2

## (H)

**half round rod handle iron**
No. 3 p. 3 fig. 12
price, No. 3 fig. 38
**Handi Works Brisbane,** No. 9 Fig. 14
**hand fluter,** *see* fluter, hand
**handles**
Enterprise
letter from Bill Davis, No. 17 p. 2
identification of country, No. 1 p. 3
**Hanson, Delores**
letter, No. 16 p. 2
**Hanson, H. C.**
patent, No. 16 fig. 8
**Harn, Pattidawn and Bill**
letter, No. 15 p. 2
**Harper**
set of 3 bases
price, No. 8 fig. 33
**hat block**
photo, No. 12 fig. 7
**hat-body former, cone for,** No. 12 p. 14
**hat irons**
cover story, "19th Century Hatter," No. 12 p. 4
**"Hatters' Glossary,"** No. 12 p. 10
**hatters' plane,** No. 12 p. 7, fig. 19
**hatters' shackle,** No. 14 fig. 46
price, No. 14 fig. 83
**hatters' shell,** No. 12 p. 6, fig. 11, 13
price, No. 12 fig. 129-131
**hatters' tools,** No. 8 p. 23 fig. 23
*See* tolliker
**Haven & Co., dolphin uprights**
price, No. 15 fig. 55
**Hawkins, Bill**
letter, No. 9 p. 2
**Headon, Rosemary and Will**
letter, No. 16 p. 2
**heater**
gas
Mora rocking. No. 7 fig. 15
price, No. 7 fig. 51
Dessau, No. 7 p. 12 fig. 64-65
price, No. 7 fig. 50
sad iron
price, No. 4 fig. 38
pyramid
photo, No. 14 fig. 4
price, No. 4 fig. 47, No. 14 fig. 72
sad iron

price, No. 4 fig. 38-49
*See also* named heater
**Helga's ABC,** No. 7 fig. 25
**Henderson, Vi and Jan**
No. 7 p. 8 fig. 20, 24
letter, No. 14 p. 2
**Herrick, Charlie Jr.,** No. 8 p. 3
**Hersch, Sterling L.**
letter, No. 9 p. 2
**Hewitt combination iron**
price, No. 16 fig. 30
**Hewitt, John,** No. 4 p. 8, *See* King Iron
**Hicks, Laura M., inventor**
No. 19 p. 14
**Hilner, Clarence and Beverly,** No.5 p. 2
**Holland,** *see* Netherlands
**hollow grip iron**
No. 3 p. 3 fig. 11
price, No. 3 fig. 39
**Holmes crank fluter**
No. 5 p. 6 fig. 24
price, No. 5 fig. 63
**Hong Kong Museum of Arts**
No. 16 p. 2
**"Hood's" patent polisher**
price, No. 8 fig. 53
**"Hotpoint Utility Iron"**
No. 6 p. 12 fig. 69-71
price, No. 6 fig. 68
**hot water iron**
"Atkins Patent"
No. 6 p. 8 fig. 22
price, No. 12 fig. 119
**Howell, Sara**
No. 15 p. 2
**"Howell Wave Fluter"**
price, No. 8 fig. 34
**Hunt, Ted**
No. 13 p. 2
**"Husqvarna,"** No. 1 p. 3, fig. 9, 41
stand, No. 1 p. 2
**Hydro-Carbon Iron, The**
No. 16 p. 7, fig. 12
advertisement
No. 16 fig. 11

## (I)

**ice cream scoops,** No. 7 p. 8
**Imperial Brass Mfg. Co.**
No. 9 fig. 23
tailor iron
price, No. 4 p. 7
**"Imperial" crank fluter**
price, No. 15 fig. 43

**"Imperial Self Heating Flat Iron"**
    photo, No. 19 fig. 23
    price, No. 9 fig. 44, No. 13 fig. 42
**"Improved Easy Iron, The,"**
    No. 9 fig. 10
    price, No. 9 fig. 45, No. 13 fig. 43, No. 16 fig. 40
**"Improved Progress Iron,"**
    No. 1 fig. 5, 45
**Incandescent Light and Supply Co.**
    No. 16. p. 5, fig. 6
**index**
    1995 No. 2 insert
    1996 No. 8 insert
    1997 No. 14 insert
**index cards**
    No. 16 p. 6
**India irons**
    charcoal irons, No. 1 fig. 8
**Indonesian irons**
      charcoal, No. 1 p. 3 figs, 11, 34
      little, No. 1 fig. 11, 35
**Ingram, Ray**
    letter, No. 13 p. 2
**inventor of the iron**
    No. 16 p. 2
**iron collecting,** *see* collecting, iron
**iron pattern,** No. 13 fig. 21, p. 14 fig. 26-31
*Irons by Irons*
    book, No. 8 p. 7, 9
**Irons, Dave**
    No. 7 fig. 28, No. 8 p. 7-9 fig. 14-15, 17, 19-20, No. 15 p. 7, fig. 9
**Irons, Sue**
    No. 8 p. 7 fig. 14, 17
**iron-shaped sprinkler**
    No. 18 fig. 16-18
    price, No. 18 fig. 65-68
    plastic, No. 18 fig. 43
**Iron Talk**
    at Atlantic City, No. 7 fig. 25-26
**Irontiques,** No. 7 p. 7 fig. 22, 25
**Isely, Bliss**
    No. 16 p. 12
**ivy, green sprinker,** No. 18 fig. 16
    price, No. 18 fig. 65

## (J)

**Jankowski, Jerry,** No. 7 p. 2
**Japan, irons**
    types
      charcoal, No. 1 fig. 6, 36
**Jasso, Gayle,** No. 6 p. 7
**"Jewel" gas iron**
    price, No. 8 fig. 48-49

**Johnson, Karlynn**
    letter, No. 9 p. 2
**Johnson, Sally**
    letter, No. 18 p. 2
**Jordan, Darlene**
    letter, No. 11 p. 2
**Joarnt, Roger**
    letter, No. 14 p. 2
**"Jubilee" iron**
    photo, No. 9 fig. 8
    price, No. 9 fig. 47, No. 13 fig. 46, No. 16 fig. 41
**Jubilee Manufacturing Co.** *See* "Jubilee" iron
**Junker & Ruth,** No. 7 p. 4

## (K)

**Kellett, Shirlee**
    No. 15 fig. 5
    letter, No. 14 p. 2
**Kelley, Dick**
    letter, No. 5 p. 2
**Kelley, Norman L.**
    letter, No. 10 p. 2, No. 15 p. 2
**Kenton Toy Co.**
    No. 20 p. 10
**"King Iron, The"**
    No. 4 p. 8-9 fig. 20-21
      price, No. 4 fig. 52
**Kinnemeyer, Babe**
    No. 15 p. 10, fig. 14
    letter, No. 5 p. 2
    photo, No. 13 fig. 14
**"Kleanser Kate" cleanser dispenser**
    No. 10 fig. 15
    price, No. 10 fig. 37-38
**K-M,** *see* "Gad-A-Bout"
**Knapp, Myron H.,** No. 4 p. 8, No. 5 p. 6
**Knapp patent,** No. 5 p. 6 fig. 23
    price, No. 5 fig. 59, No. 7 fig. 37
**Knight, Cec,** No. 4 p. 6-7 fig. 16
**Knotnerus, Hans and Herma**
    photo, No. 16 fig. 12
    "Slicken-or Rubbingstones" No. 16 p. 12
**"Knox" crank fluter**
    price, No. 15 fig. 42
**"Knox/McDonald Rotary Iron,"** No. 6 fig. 8
    price, No. 5 fig. 64, No. 7 fig. 37
**Knox, Susan,** No. 5 p. 5
**Krohn, Carole**
    letter, No. 10 p. 2
**Krohn, William**
    letter, No. 10 p. 2
**Kutztown Extravaganza,** No. 8 p. 9

# (L)

**"Ladies Friend,"** No. 4 fig. 4
  price, No. 4 fig. 53
**"Lady Bug" sprinkler**
  No. 18 fig. 22
  price, No. 18 fig. 69
**"Lady Ironing" sprinkler,** No. 18 fig. 17
  price, No. 18 fig. 66
**Lafitte, Jean,** No. 5 p. 8
**Lammerts, Mrs. S. A.**
  Letter, No. 1 p. 2
**Lancaster County Antiques & Collectible Mall**
  No. 8 p. 9
**LaRue Nu-Styl Gas Iron**
  price
    standard, No. 19 fig. 47
    w/stand and weight, No. 19 fig 48
**Latterell, Carmen**
  letter, No. 10 p. 2
  letter, No. 11 p. 2
  letter, No. 14 p. 2
**"Laundry Maid" fuel iron**
  price, No. 16 fig. 42
**"Laundry Sprinkler," plastic**
  price, No. 18 fig. 43
**"Laurel Fletcher, The,"** gas iron
  price, No. 8 fig. 49
**lead mini irons,** No. 3 fig. 64
**"Leader, New" iron**
  patent papers, No. 9 fig. 6
  photo, No. 9 fig. 6
**Le Gresley, Robert,** No. 7 p. 2
**Leighty, Jo,** letter, No. 6 p. 2
**Lenski, Jean Pierre**
  No. 20 fig. 23
**Leonard, Louise,** letter, No. 8 p. 2
**"LFB,"** No. 7 fig. 13, 17
  price, No. 7 fig. 42
**linen press,** No. 8 p. 12 fig. 59-61
  price, No. 8 fig. 47
**"Lion of St. Mark"**
  No. 15 cover and fig. 1
**little**
  entire issue, No. 3
  charcoal
    No. 1 p. 4, fig. 11-13, 35, 39, 44
    curled handle
      No. 3 p. 1 fig. 2, No. 19 fig. 2, 3
      price, No. 3 fig. 30-31, No. 4 fig. 35-36,
    No. 19 fig. 51, 52
    detachable handle iron, No. 14 fig. 37
      price, No. 14 fig. 73
    No. 19 fig. 2, 3
  fluter
    "Little Fluters" cover story

  No. 7 p. 1, 3 fig. 1-7
French iron
  price, No. 15 fig. 48
Potts type
  letter from Bill Davis, No. 16 p. 2
rod handle, No. 3 p. 3 fig. 9
  price, No. 3 fig. 45
rope handle, No. 3 p. 1 fig. 1, No. 14 fig. 27
  price, No. 3 fig. 46-47, No. 4 fig. 37, No. 14 fig. 28
round back, No. 3 p. 4 fig. 14
  price, No. 3 fig. 48
Scottish
  brass
    No. 15 cover and fig. 1
swan, No. 3 p. 3 fig. 7, No. 14 fig. 74
  price, No. 3 fig. 51-54, No. 14 fig. 75
  1¼" No. 19 fig. 10
    price, No. 19 fig. 54
  1⁵⁄₁₆" No. 19 fig. 11
    price, No. 19 fig. 55
  1¾" No. 19 fig. 12
    price, No. 19 fig. 56
  1⅞" No. 19 fig. 13
    price, No. 19 fig. 57
  1¹⁵⁄₁₆" No. 19 fig. 14
    price, No. 19 fig. 58
  2⅛" No. 19 fig. 15
    price, No. 19 fig. 59
  2³⁄₁₆" No. 19 fig. 16
    price, No. 19 fig. 60
  2¼" No. 19 fig. 17
    price, No. 19 fig. 61
  2⅜" No. 19 fig. 18
    price, No. 19 fig. 62
  2¾" No. 19 fig. 19
    price, No. 19 fig. 63
  2¾" plain No. 19 fig. 20
    price, No. 19 fig. 64
  2¾" brass No. 19 fig. 21
    price, No. 19 fig. 65
  2⅜" "Folks Fescht" No. 19 fig. 22
    price, No. 19 fig. 66
  3¼" "Rara Avis" No. 19 fig. 23
    price, No. 19 fig. 67
  3½" No. 19 fig. 24
  5" No. 19 fig. 25
    price, No. 19 fig. 68
  catalog page
    Russel and Erwin Mfg. Co.
    No. 19 fig. 4
  cover story, "Little Swan Irons,"
    No. 19 p. 4-6, fig. 1-8
  five inch
    price, No. 15 fig. 60
  "Gallery of Little Swan Irons"

No. 19. p. 6, fig. 10-25
    reproduction
        No. 16 p. 2, No. 19 p. 5, fig. 5
        price, No. 19 fig. 53
    tailor, No. 2 p. 8-9, fig. 30
    Tri-Bump, No. 3 p. 2 fig. 6
        price, No. 3 fig. 55-56
    trivet (stand)
        cathedral, No. 19 fig. 9
        price, No. 19 fig. 69
        reproduction
            Iron Art
                No. 19 fig. 6
                price, No. 19 fig. 70
    wire handle, No. 3 p. 3 fig. 8
        price, No. 3 fig. 58
*See also* classification

**"Little Giant" combination iron**
    price, No. 15 fig. 37
**Lowe, James and Marie**
    letter, No. 16 p. 2
**Lucullus,** No. 5 p. 8, 9 fig. 37
**"Lustra-Ware Clothes Sprinkler"**
    No. 18 fig. 46

## (M)

**machine (crank) fluter,** see named fluter
**Magazine**
    "Country Gentleman, The," No. 13 fig. 66
        price, No. 13 fig. 50
**Magazine Street,** No. 5 p. 8 fig. 33
**"Magic" fluting machine**
    price, No. 4 p. 7
**Mahony polisher**
    photo, No. 14 fig. 34
    price, No. 8 fig. 51, No. 14 fig. 78, No. 15 fig. 53
**mailing label,** No. 8 p. 2
**"Mammy," black, new sprinker**
    No. 10 fig. 1, 19
    price, No. 10 fig. 56
**"Mammy," black, old sprinkler,**
    No. 10 fig. 1, 19, No. 18 fig. 27
    price, No. 10 fig. 57, No. 18 fig. 70
**"Mammy, Tall," black, new sprinkler**
    No. 10 fig. 9
    price, No. 10 fig. 51
**"Mammy, Short," black, new sprinkler**
    No. 10 fig. 9
    price. No. 10 fig. 50
**"Mandy" sprinkler**
    old and new
    No. 10 fig. 1, 19
**mangle**
    "Household Clothes Mangle"
        price, No. 20 fig. 54

**mangle, electric,** No. 10 p. 2
**mangle, electric toy**
    price, No. 4 p. 7
**mangle, friction toy**
    price, No. 4 p. 7
**mangling board**
    No. 19 fig. 34, 35
    price, No. 20 fig. 55
**Mann, A. S.,** No.4 p. 4
    iron, No. 4 p. 4 fig. 9
    patent papers, No. 4 fig. 9
    price, No. 4 fig. 54
**"Manville" crank fluter**
    price, No. 7 fig. 24, 38, No. 15 fig. 41
**Markets**
    "Atlantique City," No. 7 p. 7
    "Canadian Iron Auction," No. 4 p. 6
    "Mount Dora, Florida," No. 13 p. 10
    "New Orleans," No. 5 p. 8
    "Nuevo Laredo, Mexico," No.1 p. 6
    "Round Top, Texas," No. 10 p. 8
**"Marvel"**
    stand, No. 1 p. 2
**"Mary Poppins"**
    No. 18 fig. 24
    Price, No. 18 fig. 71
**Mascieri, Russ**
    No. 11 p. 11
**"Massengill,"** No. 9 p. 2
**matchcase,** No. 3 p. 9 fig. 25A, p. 10 fig. 25Aa
    price, No. 3 fig. 40
**"Max Elb"**
    No. 1 fig. 31
    No. 20 p. 14, fig. 25
    directions for use
        No. 20 p. 15
    price, No. 20 fig. 44
**McClain Collection,** No. 3 p. 8
**McDonald's (McDonald /Knox) rotary hat iron**
    price, No. 6 fig. 55, No. 12 fig. 120
**McFarlane, J & A** hand fluter
    price, No. 16 fig. 36
**Meeker, Carole**
    No. 7 p. 8 fig. 23
    letter, No. 10 p. 2
**Mennonite,** No. 12 p4
**"Merry Maid" sprinkler**
    new colored glass
        No. 10 p. 6 fig. 14
        price, No. 10 fig. 58
    old plastic by Relaince
        No. 10 p. 6 fig. 13, No. 18 fig. 21
        price, No. 10 fig. 59, No. 18 fig. 73
**Meta Fuel iron,** No. 6 p. 3, 6 fig. 6, 7, 15

**Mexico irons**
　charcoal
　　No. 1 fig. 16-18, 20-21, 37-38
　sad
　　No. 1 fig. 17, 57-58
**Meyers**
　center latch, No. 3 p. 4 fig. 18
　　price, No. 7 fig. 57
　toy 3 W inch, No. 4 p. 7
**Midwest Sad Iron Collectors Club**
　address, No. 14 p. 5, No. 20 p. 2
　photo of sales room, No. 14 fig. 13
**miniature iron,** *see* little
**mob-cap,** No. 3 p. 8 fig. 24
**model, patent,** *see* patent model
**"Monitor, The" iron**
　photo, No.9 fig. 4, No. 14 fig. 33,
　　No. 16 fig. 20, 25
　price, No. 4 p. 7, No. 9 fig. 48, No. 14 fig. 71
　Model 5
　　price, No. 19 fig. 75
　streamlined Model A
　　price, No. 9 fig. 49
**Monitor Sad Iron Co.**
　No. 16 p. 12
　*See also,* "The Monitor" iron
**monster iron**
　"Berliner," No. 1 p. 3, fig. 9, 28, No. 6 fig. 24
　"Griffin," No. 1 p. 3, fig. 9, 30
　"Husqvarna," No. 1 p. 3, fig. 9, 41
**Montgomery Ward**
　triangle tank
　　photo, No. 9 fig. 19
　　price, No. 9 fig. 50, No. 13 fig. 45
**Moore, Linda**
　letter, No. 19 p. 2
**"Mora" heater,** No. 7 p. 6
　price. No. 7 fig. 51
**"More Irons by Irons"**
　article, No. 8 p. 7
　book, No. 8 p. 7, 9
**Mosholder, Gene and Jerry**
　letter, No. 7 p. 2
**mouth sprayer**
　No. 18 fig. 41
**"Mr. Sprinkle" plastic sprinker**
　No. 18 fig. 43
**mushroom iron**
　price, No. 20 fig. 56
**Myers**
　goat fluter
　　No. 15 cover and fig. 2
　　　price, No. 15 fig. 39

**"Myrtle" sprinkler**
　No. 18 fig. 25
　Price, No. 18 fig. 75

## (N)

**Nacker, Richard**
　letter, No. 8 p. 2
**napkin press,** No. 5 p. 9 fig. 37
　price, No. 5 fig. 72
**National Stamping Co. iron**
　photo, No. 9 fig. 25
　price, No. 8 fig. 40, No. 9 fig. 51
**National Stamping Co. Electric Works**
　photo, No. 9 fig. 25
**"Naughty Lady"** *faux* **sprinkler**
　No. 10 fig. 17
　price, No. 10 fig. 33
**needlecase**
　No. 3 p. 9, 10 fig. 25B, 25Bb
　price, No. 3 fig. 41
**neep,** No. 7 p. 3 fig. 5
　price, No. 7 fig. 59
**Ne Plus Ultra**
　No. 1 p. 10, fig. 23, 46
　price, No. 13 fig. 33
**Netherlands**
　charcoal
　　No. 1 p. 2
　stand
　　No. 1 p. 2
**"New Leader" iron**
　photo, No. 9 fig. 6
　price, No. 9 fig. 52
**"New Orleans,"** No. 5 p. 8
**New Orleans Coffee and Concierge**
　No. 5 p. 9
**nickel cleaning,** No. 8 p. 5
**"Nonpareil, The" iron**
　patent paper, No. 9 fig. 5A
　photo, No. 9 fig. 5B
　price, No. 9 fig. 53
**Nudelman, Eric**
　letter, No. 19 p. 2
**nugget,** *see* fuel, briquettes
**numbers, figure,** No. 6 p. 2

## (O)

**Ober**
　Twila and Doug
　　photo, No. 13 fig. 18
　factory, No. 6 p. 2
　irons
　　detachable handle iron, No. 14 fig. 40
　　　price, No. 14 fig. 59
　　little

No. 3 p. 3 fig. 12
    price, No. 3 fig. 38
sad iron
    photo, No. 14 fig. 30
        price, No. 14 fig. 81
sleeve iron
    price, No. 16 fig. 49
**"Oblong Waffle" stand,** No. 1 p. 2
**Ogden, Oliver**
    "19th Century Hatter" p. 4
    photo, No. 12 cover, fig. 1, 2, 8, 9
**Ogden, Sharon,**
    photo, No. 12 fig. 2, 4
**"OK Family Iron,"** No. 4 p. 3
**oldest iron**
    No. 16 p. 2
**Old Order River Brethren,** No. 12 p. 4
**"Olmsted" lever-operated fluter**
    No. 8 fig. 16
        price, No. 8 fig. 38
**"Onlyone" charcoal iron**
    No. 1 p. 10, fig. 23, 47
        price, No. 16 fig. 24
**open-rolled grip iron,** No. 3 p. 3 fig. 16
    price, No. 8 fig. 43
**Oriental mouth sprayer**
    No. 18 fig. 41
**Oscars Antiques,** No. 1 p. 6
**"Otto, Improved"**
    price, No. 16 fig. 44
**Otty, George L.**
    letter, No. 19 p. 2
**oval iron,** No. 3 p. 4

## (P)

**painting**
    Degas, No. 14 fig. 86
**paint removal,** No. 8 p. 3
**pan iron**
    China, No. 19 fig. 27
    authentication
        No. 20 p. 2
    how they were used
        No. 20 p. 2
        price, No. 20 fig. 57
**Parker, Bethany**
    letter, No. 16 p. 2
**Patent Act of 1836,** No. 4 p. 3
**"Patent History of 19th Century American Fluting Irons, A,"** No. 5 p.7
**patent model**
    bosom board
        price, No. 15 fig. 49
    reversible
        No. 4 p. 3 fig. 7

    price, No. 15 fig. 49
washing machine, No. 13 fig. 20
    price, No. 13 fig. 51
**patent papers**
    American Gas Machine, No. 16 fig. 8
    "Best Yet," No. 9 fig. 13
    "Casey, J. F. & Co.," No. 9 fig. 17
    Finn "Ne Plus Ultra, " No. 1 p. 10
    Hanson, H. C. patent, No. 16 fig. 8
    Liquid Fuel Flatiron by John Slezak, No. 9 fig. 32
    "New Leader," No. 9 fig. 6
    "Nonpareil, The," No. 9 fig. 5A
    "Peerless, The," No. 16 fig. 8
    Sears design by John Morgan, No. 9 fig. 32
    "Taliaferro & Cummings." No. 1 p. 8
**pattern, iron,** No. 13 fig. 21, p. 14 fig. 26-31
**Payne, Pete and Nancy,** No. 6 p. 8 fig. 23, 29, 31B
**Pease, H. S. Combination Charcoal Iron**
    No. 20 p. 18, fig. 33-35
        price, No. 20 fig. 46
    patent paper, No. 20 fig. 35
**"Peasant Lady" sprinkler**
    No. 18 fig. 23
    price, No. 18 fig. 76
**"Peerless, The" iron**
    advertisement
        No. 16 fig. 10
    No. 16 p. 5, fig. 5
    patent paper
        No. 16 fig. 8
    similarity to American Gas Machine Co.,
    No. 9 p. 2
    price, No. 8 fig. 37
**Peery, Karen**
    letter, No. 8 p. 2
**"Perfecto"**
    advertisement, No. 16 fp. 11, fig. 15
    patent paper, No. 16 fig. 16
    photo, No. 9 fig 19, No. 16 fig. 17
    price, No. 9 fig. 54
**Perkins patent,** *see* "Doty"
**Phillips, Bob**
    letter, No. 20 p. 2
**Phillips, Gladyce**
    letter, No. 12 p. 2
**phonograph, invention date,** No. 4 p. 1
**Picken, Bill**
    No. 15 p. 6, fig. 7
    *see also* collectors
**Picken collection**
    "Bente and Bill Picken" No. 20 p. 19
**"Pip and Squeek,"** No. 3 p. 5
**Picken, Bente,** No. 4 p. 6, 7 fig. 14
**Picken, Bill,** No. 4 p. 6, 7 fig. 14
**Pilgrim Care Center,** No. 4 p. 5

61

**plastic clothes sprinklers**
No. 18 fig. 43-46
**pleater**
pleating machine
Singer Mfg. Co., The
price, No. 15 fig. 51
wood and metal
price, No. 15 fig. 50
**poems**
"Pip and Squeek," No. 3 p. 5
"She Liked Irons," No. 6 p. 14
**Pogoel**
charcoal iron
photo, No. 14 fig. 32
price, No. 14 fig. 55
stand
No. 1 p. 2
**poking stick**
price, No. 20 fig. 58-59
**polisher**
unnamed
No. 14 fig. 25
price, No. 14 fig. 79
*see* "B.S.&R."
*see* "Gem"
*see* "Hood's patent"
*see* "Mahoney"
*see* "Mary Ann B. Cook"
*See also* named iron
**Politzer, Frank**
No. 3 p. 2, 6, 7-8 fig. 19, 22
letter, No. 5 p. 2, No. 9 p. 2, No. 13 p.2
**Politzer, Judy**
No. 3 p. 1, 6-8 fig. 19-20, No. 4 p. 12
**Ponce, Fulgencio Garcia**
letter, No. 10 p. 2
**Ponton, J,** No. 2 fig. 32, 58
**poodle sprinkler**
No. 18 fig. 30
price, No. 18 fig. 77
**pop bottle sprinkler**
price, No. 10 fig. 61
**Portugal irons**
little
No. 1 p. 3, 13, No. 3 fig. 61
price, No. 1 fig. 39, 40,  No. 3 fig. 44
**postcards**
No. 1 p. 11, No. 2 p. 11, No. 3 p. 9
Flatiron building, No. 20 fig. 3
price, No. 20 fig. 60
Flat Iron Girl, No. 20 fig. 4
price, No. 20 fig. 61
**posters,** No. 5 p. 1
**poster stamps,** No. 5 p. 1-4, 11-12 fig. 1-16
price, No. 5 p. 4 fig. 73-74, No. 7 fig. 60-61

**"Poster Stamps" cover story,**  No. 5 p. 1
**Post, Mary Sue**
letter, No. 15 p. 2
**Post, Maureen**
letter, No. 11 p. 2
**Potts irons**
advertisement, No. 11 fig. 4
description, No. 11 p. 3
handles
letter from Bill Davis, No. 16 p. 2
photographs, No. 11 fig. 3, 5
**Potts, Mrs. Florence**
"Mrs. Potts Advertising Trade Cards"
No. 11 p. 5
prices, No. 11 p. 12
"Mrs. Florence Potts: The True Story"
No. 11 p. 1
portrait, No. 11 fig. 2
**Praline Connection, The,** No. 5 p. 9
**"Prayer Lady" sprinkler**
No. 18 fig. 28
price, No. 18 fig. 78
**preservation of irons,** No. 8 p. 2
**pressed glass**
*see* Cookstove, pressed glass
*Pressing Irons and Trivets*
price
No. 20, fig. 41
**price guides,** No. 4 p. 12, No. 8 p. 7
**"Price Lists, Truth About,"** No. 4 p. 12
**prices**
No. 1 p. 11
No. 2 p. 11
No. 3 p. 11
No. 4 p. 11
No. 5 p. 11
No. 6 p. 11
No. 7 p. 11
No. 8 p. 11
No. 9 p. 11
No. 10 p. 11
No. 11 p. 12
No. 12 p. 15
No. 13 p. 15
No. 14 p. 15
No. 15 p. 15
No. 16 p. 15
No. 18 p. 15
No. 19 p. 15
No. 20 p. 19
**Priestley & Co.,** No. 1 p. 12
**products,** No. 8 p. 4
**puller down,** No. 12 p. 6, fig. 15
price, No. 12 fig. 121
**pump,** No. 9 fig. 69

## (Q)

**"Queen" sprinkler,** No. 10 fig. 2
    price, No. 10 fig. 61

## (R)

**"Radish" sprinkler,** No. 10 fig. 2
    price, No. 10 fig. 64
**Reavis, Raymond**
    No. 16 p. 3
**"Record Keeping for Iron Collectors"**
    No. 16 p. 4
**receptacle, iron**
    *see,* cooler, iron
**Renninger's,** No. 8 p. 9
**replaced handle**
    price, No 20 fig. 62
**reproduction and new**
    Dutch charcoal iron
        letter from Jean Serva, No. 16 p. 2
    *see,* sprinklers, little swans
**rest, Bunker Claney Mfg. Co.**
    price, No. 8 fig. 54
**restoration of irons,** No. 8 p. 2
**reversible iron,** *see* combination, reversible
    "Trent, The"
        price, No. 20 fig. 63
    *see also* named iron
**"Reversible Combination Irons"**
    cover story, No. 4 p. 1
**revolving iron,** *see* reversible
**rod handle,** *see* little
**Rogowski, Lila**
    letter, No. 9 p. 2
**"Rooster" sprinkler**
    No. 10 p. 5 fig. 11, No. 18 fig. 32
    price, No. 10 fig. 63, No. 18 fig. 79
**"Rooster" iron-shaped sprinkler**
    No. 18 fig.. 17
    price, No. 18 fig. 66
**rope handle**
    *see,* little
**Rosengren, G. T.**
    patent, No. 16 fig. 16
**Rosen, Sam**
    letter, No. 11 p. 2
**rotary iron,** No. 7 p. 9-10 fig. 27, 29
    price, No. 7 fig. 62
**round back iron,** *see* little
**rounding jack,** No. 12 p. 7, fig. 16
    price, No. 12 fig. 122
**Round Top, Texas,** No. 10 p. 8
**Round Top Cafe**
    No. 10 p. 9
**Rousseau, Bernie,** No. 8 p. 4
**Royal Bayreuth,** No. 6 p. 9 fig. 30

    price, No. 6 fig. 41-42
**Royal iron**
    No. 16 p. 12 13, fig. 20
    front tank
        No. 16 fig. 20
        price, No.4 p. 7, No. 9 fig. 56
    Model D
        price, No. 9 fig. 55
**Royal Street,** No. 5 p. 8 fikg. 36
**rubber bulb sprinker,** *see* bulb (rubber)
**Rudolph, Kay**
    letter, No. 13 p. 2
**Rueckert Mfg. Co.,** No. 6 p. 2
**Rue de la Course,** No. 5 p. 8
**Ruiz. Maria Teresa Esque**
    letter, No. 15 p. 2
**runner down,** No. 12 p. 6, fig. 10
    price, No. 12 fig. 123-124
**rust removal,** No. 8 p. 3

## (S)

**saccarine container**
    No. 3 p. 9, 10 fig. 25C, 25Cc
    price, No. 3 fig. 42
**sad/fluter**
    *see* maker's name
    *see* combination irons, sad/fluter
**sad iron**
    No. 5 fig. 35
    price, No. 5 75-77
    Belgium
        price, No. 15 fig. 54
    France
        No. 14 fig. 38
        price, No. 14 fig. 80
    set of five
        price, No. 15 fig. 56
    history, No. 1 p. 1
    meaning, No. 14 p. 2, 10
        price, No. 14 fig. 82
    pressed glass, No. 2 p. 6-7, fig. 20-24, 63-64
    "Ton of Irons, A," No. 19 p. 13 fig. 41-42
    unmarked, No. 14 fig.18
    *see also,* named iron
**Salesman sample,** No.12 p. 2
**salt shaker**
    No.20 fig. 22
**Sauerbier machine fluter,** No. 12 p. 2
**Schenkemeyer, Jr. Esq., C. D.**
    letter, No. 15 p. 2
**Schravesande, Bitsy and Art**
    letter, No. 18 p. 2
    No. 18 p. 3
**Scotten Dillon Co.** *see* Tobacco cutter

**Scottish box iron**
No. 6 fig. 27, No. 13 p. 13 fig. 22-25
"The Apprentice's Test Piece," No. 23 p. 4
price, No. 4 p. 7, No. 8 fig. 57, No. 13 fig. 52-57
**"Secrets of Cleaning Irons"**
cover story No. 8 p. 1
**Seeley, H. W.**
inventor of electric iron
No. 16 p. 2
**"Sensible"**
detachable handle
Sensible No. 4
No. 14 fig. 31
price, No. 4 p. 7
sleeve iron
Sensible No. 4
price, No. 13 fig. 58
Sensible No. 5
price, No. 1 fig. 59
price, No. 13 fig. 59
**Sersch, Sterling L.**
letter, No. 15 p. 2
**Serva, Jean**
letter, No. 16 p. 2
**"Sette, The"**
No. 9 fig. 24
price, No. 8 fig. 39, No. 9 fig. 59
**Schnitizius, Cindy**
letter, No. 14 p. 2
**Scottish Box Iron**
"Apprentice's Test Piece, The," No. 13 p. 4
arrowhead "S" supports, No. 13 fig. 1
price, No. 13 fig. 52
baluster uprights, No. 13 fig. 5
little, No. 13 fig. 9
price, No. 13 fig. 57
catalog sheet, No. 13 fig. 11
Gothic "S," No. 13 fig. 6
price, No. 13 fig. 53
group of six, No. 19 fig. 38
rotating handle, No. 13 p. 13, fig. 22
price, No. 13 fig. 55
separating at sole, No. 19 fig. 30
shaped strap, brass & copper grip,
No. 13 fig. 4
price, No. 13 fig. 56
"S" supports, amber glass grip, No. 13 fig. 3
"S" supports, plain, No. 13 fig. 8
price, No. 13 fig. 54
**Sears irons**
Model No. 2435, No. 9 fig. 29
Model No. 5947, No. 9 fig. 30
price, No. 9 fig. 57, No. 13 fig. 46
Model No. 5988, No. 9 for. 31
price, No. 9 fig. 58

"Wonder Gasoline Iron, The," No. 9 p. 9 fig. 29, 32
**self-heating irons**
*See* fuel irons
**Sette**
photo, No. 9 fig. 24
price, No. 9 fig. 59
**shakers, salt and pepper**
Dutch Boy and Girl, No. 10 fig. 16
price, No. 10 fig. 41
**shackle,** No. 12 p. 7, fig. 23
price, No. 12 fig. 125-128
**Sharp, J. L. and Luther, J. D.**
patent, No. 6 p. 5
**"She Liked Irons," poem,** No. 6 p. 7
**shell,hatters',** No. 12 p. 6, fig. 11, 13
price, No 12 fig. 129-131
**Shimer, Milton J.**
price, No. 4 p. 7
**"siamese cat" sprinkler**
No. 18 fig. 33
price, No. 18 fig. 80
**Silagyi, Carol**
letter, No. 6 p. 2
**Silver Streak**
price, No. 15 fig. 40
**"Simplex Ironer,"** No. fig. 12
**Sims, Dan**
letter, No. 18 p. 2
**Sinclair, Darlene and L. G.**
letter, No. 5 p. 2, No. 16 p. 2
**Sinclair, L. G.**
No. 15 p. 10, fig. 13
**Sinclair/Kohler collection**
No. 20 fig. 9, 10
**"Six Flags" sprinkler**
No. 18 fig. 18
price, No. 18 fig. 67
**slant handle iron**
Acorn Brass Mfg. Co.
advertising, No. 9 fig. 2
iron, No. 9 fig. 2
price, No. 9 fig. 60
**slave iron**
No. 1 fig. 59, No. 20 p. 2
**sleeve iron**
duckbill
price, No. 15 fig. 58
electric
price, No. 16 gig. 48
set of two
price, No. 15 fig. 59
*See* named iron
**slickenstone**
No. 15 p. 12, 14, fig. 17, 24-27
No. 16 p. 12, fig. 11, 13-17

**"Slickenstone-or Rubbingstones"**
No. 16 p. 12
**slip stick,** No. 12 p. 7, fig. 18
**"Smallest of the Small,"** No. 3 p. 12
**small irons,** *see* little
**Smallwood, Jeanette**
letter, No. 14 p. 2
**Smock, Howard**
letter, No. 16 p. 2
**Smothers, Steve**
No. 18 p. 3
**soap**
photo, No. 14 fig. 12
**soapstone iron**
price, No. 19 fig. 76
**soft drink bottle sprinkler**
No. 18 fig. 15
**Sour, Mr. & Mrs. Richard**
letter, No. 11 p. 2
**sources for products,** No. 8 p. 5
**souvenir salt shaker**
*see* salt shaker, souvenir
**souvenir spoon**
*see* spoon, souvenir
**souvenir stein**
*see* stein, souvenir
**souvenir sprinkler**
No. 18 fig. 18
price, No. 18 fig. 67
**Spanish irons**
No. 1 p. 3
price, No. 3 fig. 49, 64
**"Special Gas Irons,"** No. 7 p. 4
**"Spider Web" stand**
No. 1 p. 2, 10, fig. 24, 60
**split chimney charcoal iron**
No. 16 fig. 29
**spoon, souvenir**
Flatiron building
No. 20 fig. 15-20
price, No. 20 fig. 64
**sprayers, clothes,** No. 10 fig. 7, No. 18 fig. 5, 6
price, No. 10 fig. 42-44, No. 18 fig. 54
**spring dent clamp,** No. 12 p. 8, fig. 25
**sprinkle bottles**
*See* sprinklers
**sprinker cap,** No. 10 fig. 5, 6
price, No. 10 fig. 45-48
**sprinkler**
No. 2 p. 8, No. 6 p. 8 fig. 28
cover story, "Clothes Sprinklers" No. 18
p. 1
cover story, "Not Quite Sprinklers" No. 10 p.1
prices, No. 10 p. 11, No. 18 p. 15
advertisements, No. 18 fig. 7

definition, No. 10 p. 3
new and reproduced
by Gale Gerds, No. 10 fig. 9
by S. Roberts Ceramics, No. 18 fig. 20
*See also,* named sprinklers
**sprinkling can,** No. 4 p. 7
**"Standard" iron**
flat tank
advertisement, No. 9 p. 4
photo, No. 9 fig. 11
price, No. 9 fig. 61, No. 13 fig. 47
freeform tank
photo, No. 9 fig. 16
price, No. 9 fig. 62
**stands**
No. 1 p. 2, 10, fig. 24, 60
brass
price, No. 20 fig. 66-67
little
Williams, No. 13 fig. 31
price, No. 13 fig. 60
Pease trivet, No. 20 p. 16, 18 fig. 32-35
price, No. 20 fig. 68
**stand,** *see* rest
**Stanford-Binet Test irons,** No. 3 p. 12 fig. 68
**Stark, Leonard,** No. 5 p 3-4
**steamer**
tube steamer, No. 4 p. 9, 10 fig. 22,
23A&B
price, No. 4 fig. 57
**steam irons**
confusion with fuel irons, No. 9 p. 3
**steam pan,** No. 12 p. 5, fig. 8
**"Steemco Steemette, Ther New"**
No. 6 p. 7 fig. 18
price, No. 6 fig. 51
**stein, souvenir**
Flatiron building, No. 20 fig. 21
**stereoscopic cards**
Flatiron building, No. 20 fig. 6-10
price, No. 20 fig. 65
**Sterling patent,** *see* "Geneva" fluter
**Sterling, Royal R.**
No. 16 p. 12, 13
**Stevens, Robert J.**
letter, No. 18 p. 2
**Stieg, Dr. Phillio & Rosemary**
letter, No. 16 p. 2
**Stoll, Pat**
letter, No. 16 p. 2
**"Story behind *Tuesday's Children,* The"**
No. 3 p. 6
**Story, S. L.**
patent model, No. 4 p. 3 fig. 7
patent papers, No. 4 fig. 8

65

**stove**

French laundry, No. 6 fig. 26

French 24-inch

price, No. 20 fig. 53

**stove, little**

Bucks Junior

price, No. 16 fig. 50

English laundry, No. 3 p. 12 fig. 60

**strap handle iron**

No. 3 p. 3 fig. 10

price, No. 3 fig. 50

**Stratton, Ethel M.**

letter, No. 7 p. 2, No. 10 p. 2

**Streeter, Jim**

letter, No. 9 p. 2

**Streeter patent**

No. 5 p. 6 fig. 25

price, No. 5 fig. 57, No. 8 fig. 30

**stretcher,** No. 12 p. 7, fig. 23

**suitcase iron**

No. 6 p. 7, 10 fig. 20, 33

price, No. 6 fig. 65

**"Sultana Toilet Iron"**

No. 6 p. 5 fig. 11A

price, No. 6 fig. 66

**"Sun" iron**

photo, No. 9 fig. 9

price, No. 9 fig. 63, No. 13 fig. 48

**"Sunbeam"**

No. 6 fig. 14

price, No. 6 fig. 46

**"Sundry" fluter**

price, No. 8 fig. 35

**Sun Flame,** price No. 19 fig. 49

**"Sunshine Iron, The"**

letterhead, No. 16 fig. 21

photo, No. 16 p. 12, fig. 18, 19, 25

**Sunshine Safety Lamp Co.**

No. 16 p. 13

letterhead, No. 16 fig. 21

**swan iron,** *see* little irons

**"Swan-on-Swan"**

No. 8 p. 7 fig. 19

price, No. 8 fig. 58

**Swanson, Vi,** No. 8 p. 2

**Sweden, irons**

charcoal, No. 1 p. 3, figs, 9, 41

**Swiss sad iron**

single post

price, No. 19 fig. 77

**Sylvester #6**

price, No. 20 fig. 42

# (T)

**tailor iron,** *see,* named iron

**"Tailgates"** cover story, No. 2 p. 1

**"Taliaferro & Cummings"**

No. 1 p. 8, fig. 49

**tanks**

cover story, "Tanks for the Memories"

No. 9 p. 1

discussion of terms, No. 9 p. 1

locations, No. 9 fig. 3

shapes

acorn, No. 9 fig. 12A

Coleman style, No. 9 fig. 12D

cylinder, No. 9 fig. 4

elongated ball, No. 9 fig. 12E

freeform, No. 9 fig. 12B

half ball, No. 9 fig. 12F

modified triangle, No. 9 fig. 12H

perfect, No. 9 fig. 12C

triangle, No. 9 fig. 12G

**Tanner, Leroy**

No. 18 p. 3

**Taute, Hazel**

letter, No. 16 p. 2

**"10 Most Frequent Mistakes"** No. 14 p. 7

**Thompson, Nancy**

letter, No. 6 p. 2

**"Thor Automatic Cladiron,"** No. 10 p. 2

**Tilley iron**

photo, No. 9 fig. 22

price, No. 9 fig. 64, No. 16 fig. 43

**"Toastmaster"**

price, No. 6 fig. 52

**tobacco cutter, Scotten Dillon Co.**

No. 2 fig. 31

price

No. 2 fig. 66

**"Toilet Smoothing Iron"** *see* Chalfant

**tolliker,** No. 12, p. 6, fig. 12, 14

price, No. 12 fig. 132-141

**tolliker, foot**

No. 8 p. 6, 10 fig. 11, 22-24

price, No. 8 fig. 43-46

**Tonnekreek, W. F. van der**

No. 7 p. 4, No. 15 fig. 16

letter, No. 9 p. 2

**"Ton of Irons, A,"** No. 19 p. 13

**toy**

*see* little

see maker's name

**Trade cards**

Enterprise trade cards

"Mrs. Potts Advertising Trade Cards"

No. 11 p. 5, fig. 6-96

prices

No. 11 p. 12

hat, No. 12 fig. 27, 108

Mclaughlin's Coffee, No. 2 p. 5
    prices
        No. 2 p. 67
**travel iron,** *see* named iron
    "Travel Irons" cover story, No. 6 p. 1
    prices, No. 6 p. 11
**"Trent, The" reversible gas iron**
    price, No. 20 fig. 63
**Tri-Bump iron,** *see* little irons
**trivet,** *see* stand
    book
        letter from Larry Bennett, No. 19 p. 2
**trousers press**
    "Empire"
        price, No. 20 fig. 69
**"Truth About Price Lists,"** No. 4 p. 12
**tube steamer,** No. 4 p. 9, 10 fig. 22, 23
**"Tucker" crank fluter**
    price, No. 16 fig. 34
**Tucker, Mrs. Arthur**
    letter, No. 9 p. 2
*Tuesday's Children*
    ordering information, No. 3 p. 7
        "*Tuesday's Children* Classification" cover story,
        No. 3 p. 1
**"Tures Mfg. Co." iron**
    similarity to American Gas Machine Co.,
        No. 9 p.2
**"Twenty-Three Skiddoo"**
    No. 20 p. 6
**two-handled gas hat iron**
    price, No. 12 fig. 142

### (U)

**"Universal Electric Travel Iron"**
    No. 6 fig. 2
    price, No. 6 fig. 54

### (V)

**valentine, comic,** No. 9 fig. 28, p. 10 fig. 33, 34
    price, No. 9 fig. 67
**valentine, iron related**
    photo, No. 9 fig. 34
    price, No. 9 fig. 68
**van der Veen**
    Jaap, No. 2 p. 10
    Lucie, No. 2 p. 10
**ventilated slotted handle**
    price, No. 19 fig. 78
**"Victor, The,"** No. 3 p. 4 fig. 17, No 4 p. 3
    price, No. 3 fig. 59
**Von Berg, Marlene**
    letter, No. 13 p. 2
**Von Berg, Marlene and Darrell**
    No. 18 p. 3

**"Vulkan"**
    No. 1 p. 5, fig. 14, 32

### (W)

**Walker, Carol**
    No. 3 p. 6 fig. 19, No. 7 fig. 26, No. 10 fig. 18, 26,
    No. 15 fig. 2, fig. 10, No. 19. fig. 41
**Walker, Alan**
    letter, No. 15 p. 2
**Walker, Jimmy**
    No. 7 fig. 26, No. 15 fig. 11
**Walsh, Darlene**
    No. 18 p. 3
**Wards**
    *See* Montgomery Ward
**washing,** No. 8 p. 3
**washing machine**
    "Columbia Washer," little
        price, No. 16 fig. 51
**wash mitt,** No. 19 p.13, 14 fig. 43-45
    price, No. 19 fig. 79
**Webb, Chuck**
    No. 11 p. 11
**wetter-downer**
    Dutch Girl, No. 10 fig. 16
        price, No. 10 fig. 65
    iron-shaped, No. 18 fig. 19
        price, No. 18 fig. 68
**Whatsit?**
    block press, No. 5 p. 7, 10 fig. 32, 40-43
    charcoal iron grate, No. 1 p. 3, 4, fig. 10
    comic valentine, No. 9 fig. 28, p. 10 fig. 33, 34
    cone for hat-body former, No. 12 p. 14
    foot tolliker, No. 8 p. 6, 10 fig. 11, 22-24
    fluting fork, No. 16 fig. 9, p. 11 fig. 10
    goffering machine, No. 10, fig. 28, p. 10 fig. 29-31
    goffering pin, No. 2 p. 5, 10, fig. 16, 33-34
    grate, charcoal, No. 1 p. 3-4, fig. 10
    iron cooler, No. 14 fig. 14, p. 14 fig. 48-51
    iron pattern, No. 13 fig. 21, p. 14 fig. 26-31
    matchcase, No. 3 p. 9, 10, fig. 25A, 25Aa
    needlecase, No. 3 p. 9, 10 fig. 25B, 25Bb
    rotary iron, No. 7 p. 9, 10 fig. 27, 29
    saccharine container, No. 3 p. 9, 10 fig. 25C, 25Cc
    slickenstone, No. 15 p. 12 fig. 17, p. 14 fig.24-27
    suitcase iron, No. 6 p. 7, 10 fig. 20, 33-34
    trivet for H. S. Pease combination iron, No. 20 p. 16,
    18, fig. 32-35
    tube steamer, No. 4 p. 9, 10 fig. 22, 23
    wash mitt, No. 19 p.13, 14 fig. 43-45
**Wheeler, Wayne**
    No. 10 fig. 26, No. 18 p. 3
**White, Suzanne,**
    letter, No. 12 p. 2
    letter, No. 14 p. 2

**Wieda,** No. 7 fig. 23
    price, No. 7 fig. 63
**Wiesehan, Ralph**
    No. 15 p. 10, fig. 51
**Wiesehan collection**
    No. 20 fig. 14, 18, 20
**Wiggins, Thomas E.**
    No. 16 fig. 7
**Williams, Jessie,** No. 7 p. 7
**wire handle,** *see* little irons
**Wolton, Jerry**
    No. 15 p. 7 fig. 12
**"Wonder Cave" sprinkler**
    No. 18 fig. 18
    price, No. 18 fig. 67
**"Wonder Gasoline Iron, The,"**
    photo, No. 9 p. 9 fig 29, 32
    price, No. 9 fig. 65
**"Wonder, The"**
    price, No. 9 fig. 66
**wood pattern**
    sleeve iron, No. 13 fig. 29
        price, No. 13 fig. 63
    top plate, No. 13 fig. 26, 27
        price, No. 13 fig. 61, 62
    trivet, No. 13 fig. 31
        price, No. 13 fig. 65
    two piece, No. 13 fig. 30
        price, No. 13 fig. 64
**Wrights (English manufacturer)**
    No. 7, p. 6 fig. 19

## (X)

## (Y)

**Young, Hewitt & Money**
    fluting board, No. 4 p. 9 fig. 21
    iron, No. 4 p. 5 fig. 12
    patent model, No. 4 p. 5 fig. 12
    patent papers, No. 4 p. 5 fig. 11

## (Z)

**Zerkle, Donna**
    letter, No. 13 p. 2

# Back issues are still available.
# $7 each, postpaid.

## Binder $7.00 plus $1.50 shipping.

For delivery to Texas address, please add 7.75% tax.

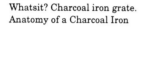

### Issue No. 1 Contents

Charcoal Irons, fire in the belly
Little Irons, mother and child
Postcards
Featured Iron: Vulcan
Markets: Nuevo Laredo
The Case of the Disappearing Chimneys
Prices
Whatsit? Charcoal iron grate.
Anatomy of a Charcoal Iron

### Issue No. 5 Contents

Poster Stamps, The forgotten collectible
Whatsit? Block press.
American Fluting Irons
Candy Containers
Markets: New Orleans
Prices
Featured Iron: American Beauty

### Issue No. 2 Contents

Box Irons, tailgates
Whatsit? Box iron with goffering pin.
Tradecards
The Truth about Pressed Glass
Collectors: Eloise Evans
Prices
Featured Iron: porcelain handle
1995 Index

### Issue No. 6 Contents

Travel Irons
She Liked Irons, poem
Featured Iron: Hotpoint Utility
Whatsit? Suitcase iron
Prices
Collectors: Pete and Nancy Payne

### Issue No. 3 Contents

The Tuesday's Children Classification
Pip and Squeek, poem
The Story Behind *Tuesday's Children*
Featured Iron: English Cap
Whatsit? Novelty little irons.
Prices
Postcards
Smallest of the Small

### Issue No. 7 Contents

Little Fluters
Special Gas Irons
Markets: Atlantique City
Whatsit? Rotary iron
Prices
Featured Iron: Rocking Gas Heater

### Issue No. 4 Contents

Reversible Combination Irons
Fingerman's Collection on TV
Canadian Iron Auction
Featured Iron: The King Iron
The Truth About Price Lists
Prices
Whatsit? Tube steamer

### Issue No. 8 Contents

Secrets of Cleaning Irons
Whatsit? Foot tolliker
More Irons by Irons
Prices
Featured Iron: Linen Press
1996 Index

### Issue No. 9 Contents

Tanks for the Memories
Whatsit? Comic valentine
Featured Iron: The Wonder Iron
Prices
Anatomy of a Fuel Iron

### Issue No. 14 Contents

Basic Iron Collection
Whatsit? Iron cooler
1997 Index
Featured Iron: Coleman 4-A
The Core Collection
Prices

### Issue No. 10 Contents

Not Quite Sprinklers
Markets: Round Top, Texas
Whatsit? Goffering machine
Prices
Featured Iron: Brittany Charcoal

### Issue No. 15 Contents

Advanced Iron Collecting
Whatsit? Slickenstone
Featured Iron: Viking Horse
Prices

### Issue No. 11 Contents

Mrs. Florence Potts: The True Story
Mrs. Potts Advertising Trade Cards
Prices

### Issue No. 16 Contents

Record Keeping for Iron Collectors
Whatsit? Fluting fork
Category Codes
Slicken-or-Rubbingstones
Prices

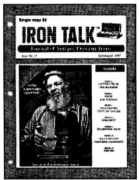

### Issue No. 12 Contents

Nineteenth Century Hatter
Whatsit? Hat body former
Featured Iron: Crown Iron
Illustrated Hatters' Glossary
Prices

### Issue No. 17 Contents

Early Coleman Irons

### Issue No. 13 Contents

The Apprentice's Test Piece
Markets: Mount Dora, Florida
Whatsit? Iron pattern
Featured Iron: Scottish Box Iron
Prices

### Issue No. 18 Contents

Clothes sprinklers
Prices

**Issue No. 19 Contents**

Little Swan Irons
Gallery of Little Swan Irons
Collectors: Bente and Bill Picken
A Ton of Irons
Whatsit? Wash mitt
Prices

**Issue No. 20 Contents**

Flatiron Building Collectibles
The Glowing Fuel Iron
Whatsit? Trivet for Pease Combination
Prices

# Subscribe: mail or phone toll-free

# IRON TALK®

### Journal of Antique Pressing Irons

## One Year — 6 issues
## $30.00 in US

Airmail delivery outside US:
$35 Canada, Mexico     $40 Other

**A must for dealers.**
**In-depth information.**
**Prices.**
**Identification.**
**Markets.**
**Where to buy and sell.**
**Trade cards.**
**What to look for.**
**Facts.**
**Where to find irons.**

**A must for collectors.**
**Patents.**
**Displaying irons.**
**Collectibles.**
**Avoid mistakes.**
**Postcards.**
**Care of irons.**
**Collectors.**
**Learn values.**
**History.**

www.irontalk.com

Send your name and address
with payment in US funds to

**IRON TALK®**
PO Box 68
Waelder TX 78959
USA

Visa and MasterCard accepted.

Order toll free
**1-800-532-IRON**

A one-year bimonthly subscription (6 issues) is $30.00.
Airmail delivery to Canada and Mexico $35. Other countries $40.
For delivery to a Texas address, add $2.33 state tax.

Carol Walker and Jimmy Walker

editors and publishers.

# Back issues: $7 each, postpaid.

# Binders: $7.00 plus $1.50 shipping.

Send your name and address
with payment in US funds to

**IRON TALK®**
PO Box 68
Waelder TX 78959
USA

Visa and MasterCard accepted.

Order toll free
**1-800-532-IRON**

# Tear-out subscription order form.

**Have fun and learn about irons. Subscribe to IRON TALK. Don't miss a single issue. Tear out this page and send it with your payment and mailing address.**

### Journal of Antique Pressing Irons

## One Year — 6 issues
## $30.00 in US
Airmail delivery outside US:
$35 Canada, Mexico.   $40 Other

A must for dealers.
In-depth information.
Prices.
Identification.
Markets.
Where to buy and sell.
Trade cards.
What to look for.
Facts.
Where to find irons.

A must for collectors.
Patents.
Displaying irons.
Collectibles.
Avoid mistakes.
Postcards.
Care of irons.
Collectors.
Learn values.
History.

www.irontalk.com

Cut on dotted line and mail with remittance to

**IRON TALK ®**
PO Box 68
Waelder TX 78959
USA

Order toll free
**1-800-532-IRON**

Your name and mailing address:

Card number . . . . . . . . . . . . . . . . . . . . . . . . .
VISA  MasterCard                Ex. Date . . . . . .

A one-year bimonthly subscription (6 issues) is $30.00.
Airmail delivery to Canada and Mexico $35.  Other countries $40.
For delivery to a Texas address, add $2.33 state tax.